# Citizenship, Inclusion and Democracy

# Citizenship, Inclusion and Democracy

## A Symposium on Iris Marion Young

*Edited by*
**Mitja Sardoč**

**Blackwell**
Publishing

First published as a special issue of *Educational Philosophy and Theory*, 2006

BLACKWELL PUBLISHING
350 Main Street, Malden, MA 02148-5020, USA
9600 Garsington Road, Oxford OX4 2DQ, UK
550 Swanston Street, Carlton, Victoria 3053, Australia

First published 2006 by Blackwell Publishing Ltd

*Library of Congress Cataloging-in-Publication Data has been applied for*

ISBN 1-4051-5601-5
ISBN 13 978-1-4051-5601-1

A catalogue record for this title is available from the British Library.

For further information on
Blackwell Publishing, visit our website:
www.blackwellpublishing.com

MIX
Paper from
responsible sources
FSC® C013604

# Contents

# Foreword

**Special Issue: Iris Marion Young**
**Guest Editor: Mitja Sardoč**

The journal welcomes this issue on the work of Iris Marion Young who is Professor of Political Science at the University of Chicago and one of the leading political thinkers on theories of justice; democracy, inclusion and difference; feminist philosophy; and, ethics and international affairs. Her books, especially *Justice and the Politics of Difference* (Princeton University Press, 1990), *Throwing Like a Girl and Other Essays in Feminist Philosophy and Social Theory* (Indiana University Press, 1990), and *Inclusion and Democracy* (Oxford University Press, 2000) have been warmly received and inspired a new generation of thinkers.

Iris Marion Young is no stranger to this journal. An interview with her (by Mitja Sardoč and Michael Shaughnessy) appeared in volume 33 (no 1, pp. 95–101) which provided a brief introduction to her and her work. There she clarified her undertaking in *Justice and the Politics of Difference* as one of criticizing the dominant paradigm of distributive justice and discussed the relations between education and justice, recognizing two aspects—the economic and political policy context (including issues of jurisdiction, segregation etc.) and the question of learning (for example, multiculturalism). This was only a brief interview that centered on her then major work on justice. In this issue six scholars in the field of education and politics discuss her work and Young willingly responds, focusing on the key questions of distributive justice in education, the irreducibility of justice to distribution, normalization, the inclusion of marginalized groups in economic and democratic processes, the tensions of 'freedom of expression' and 'tolerance' with inclusive democracy and the question of transnational education.

Her critique of the distributive paradigm highlights the increasing significance of issues of self and identity particularly in relation to Enlightenment notions of a universal stable, unchanging and essentialist self that has served as the core of Euro-American conceptions of the citizen-subject. In this context we might talk of a deepening of democracy and a political critique of Enlightenment values based upon criticism of the ways that modern liberal democracies constructs political identity. The major problem is that both liberal and Marxist theory constructs identity in terms of a series of binary oppositions (e.g., we/them, citizen/alien, responsible/irresponsible, legitimate/illegitimate) that has the effect of excluding or 'othering' some groups of people. Western countries grant rights to citizens—rights that are dependent upon citizenship—and regard non-citizens, that is, immigrants, those seeking asylum, and refugees, as 'aliens'. The political critique of the Enlightenment demands that we examine how these boundaries are socially constructed, and how they are maintained and policed. It suggests that we must learn how these boundaries are manipulated and represented in the service of political ends—witness the present attempts by neoconservatives to link and put the questions of immigration and security at the centre of the centre of public policy, especially following 9/11. The deconstruction of political hierarchies of value comprising binary oppositions and philosophies of difference, are highly significant for current debates on multiculturalism and feminism in education, as these essay demonstrate and Young's work offers a way forward that is both forceful and instructive.

The exclusion of groups from citizen status also can take place within the nation-state where a set of historic 'we/they' oppositions are used legally and politically to exclude, deny or downgrade 'rights' of minorities based on ethnicity, sexual orientation, age or disability. What Young's approach (and poststructuralist theory) allows is a better understanding of the mechanisms by which traditional exclusions have occurred and a better understanding of the centrality of questions of identity at level of the personal and individual, the community and state. Her approach promotes an understanding of the *negotiated* character of identity especially in relation to the notion of the citizen and the changing constellation of the nation-state—both after all relatively recent historical phenomena.

Political philosophy is often eclipsed in philosophy of education at the expense of ethics (can they be easily separated?) and epistemology. Little in the way of Continental political philosophy finds its way into philosophy of education conferences or journals, although this is changing especially as the community of scholars becomes more diverse and genuinely representative of global civil society. As editor of *Educational Philosophy and Theory* I welcome further essays, symposia and special issues on political philosophy in education and related issues.

Michael A. Peters
*University of Illinois at Urbana-Champaign*

# Introduction

MITJA SARDOČ

*Educational Research Institute, Ljubljana, Slovenia*

Ever since antiquity, political ideas have had a decisive influence on theorizing about education. 'Political philosophy and the philosophy of education', as Yael Tamir emphasized succinctly, 'were born together in Plato's *Republic*, and their fates have remained entwined' (Tamir, 2003, p. 501). On the other hand, different educational issues discussed by Locke, Rousseau, Kant, Mill and—more recently—by, e.g. Dewey, Oakeshott and Foucault, played an important role in their philosophical inquiries.

During the last two decades normative theorizing in educational theory has been particularly invigorated by the increasing attention political philosophers devoted to education. These debates have had a profound impact on normative theorizing about education and some of the previously neglected areas in both fields have come to dominate the center stage in terms of theory, research, policy and practice. These include issues about supporting a publicly mandated system of education which is open to all students within a particular society regardless of their particular differentiating characteristics and the development of equitable provision for diverse groups of the student population in public schools, the increasing preference for supporting pupils in gaining access and participating on increasingly equal terms in mainstream educational institutions, the civic purposes of public schooling in a culturally plural society and the issue of giving equal recognition to group identities in curriculum design.

This special issue of *Educational Philosophy and Theory* brings together six papers that engage in particular detail with the work of Iris Marion Young, one of the leading contemporary political philosophers whose theorizing and critical social analysis has sparked considerable interest in political philosophy, feminist political theory and critical social theory. Ever since the publication of her widely acclaimed book *Justice and the Politics of Difference* (1990) and her article 'Polity and Group Difference: A Critique of the Ideal of Universal Citizenship' (1989) she has gained the status of an important reference point across different disciplines associated with education: e.g. philosophy of education (Callan, 1998; Griffiths, 1995), education policy (Howe, 1997), sociology of education (Arnot & Dillabough, 2000), multicultural education (Fullinwider, 1995; 2003), feminist pedagogy (Stone, 2001), citizenship education (Macedo, 2000; Ollsen, 2001) and disability studies.

The contributors to this special issue explore aspects of conceptual as well as empirical significance in her work on differentiated citizenship, group-based politics, social justice, difference, democracy, equality and inclusion with a particular focus on the educational import of these issues. The opening contribution by Avigail Eisenberg examines the key contributions of Iris Young to democratic political theory, and the challenges that have arisen in response to Young's theory in relation to education. Elizabeth Frazer's article offers an interpretive analysis of some salient elements of Iris Young's theory of politics and then develops further what this theory of politics suggests relative to political education and education for citizenship. The contribution by Ronald Beiner starts with a critical examination of her well known concept of *differentiated citizenship* as the best way to realize the inclusion and participation of everyone in full citizenship. He then points to a number of familiar objections to Young's overall political project. Despite a critical examination of how Young's concept of group-differentiated citizenship plays out with respect to possible conflicts between contemporary multiculturalism and citizenship he emphasizes that one needs to acknowledge that Iris Young's political prescriptions offer an interesting and provocative alternative vision of what citizenship might look like in modern societies faced with social, cultural, religious and ethical diversity as the major sources of possible division of a political community. The contribution by Penny Enslin focuses on the implications of Young's views on democracy and social justice, and their implications for education under conditions of growing global inequality. Sharon Gewirtz's article builds upon Young's formulation of justice to emphasize the contextual character of contemporary political, sociological and educational debates on social justice and then offers a concrete example to illustrate these points. Finally, Simone Galea takes up Young's notions of asymmetric reciprocity and gift giving to raise some questions within the educational context of the classroom and the ethical relationships between the teacher and the student. This symposium concludes with a reply from Iris Marion Young in which she addresses the many different but related concerns by drawing up a set of questions which she sees as central to the most important issues that have been raised in the contributions to this symposium on her work.

Together, these articles form a set of theoretically illuminating discussions on one of the leading contemporary political philosophers and the educational import of her theoretical work and critical social analysis as well as a rich and diverse set of interdisciplinary contributions about the centrality of publicly provided education for disputes about citizenship, inclusion and democracy in contemporary modern pluralistic societies.

## References

M. Arnot & J. A. Dillabough (eds) (2000) *Challenging Democracy: International Perspectives on Gender, Education and Citizenship* (London, RoutledgeFalmer).

Callan, E. (1998) The Politics of Difference and Common Education. In D. Carr (ed.), *Education, Knowledge and Truth: Beyond the Postmodern Impasse* (London, Routledge).

Fullinwider, R. (1995) Citizenship, Individualism, and Democratic Politics. *Ethics*, 105:3 pp. 497–515.

Fullinwider, R. (2003) Multicultural Education, in: R. Curren (ed.), *A Companion to the Philosophy of Education* (London, Blackwell) pp. 487–500.

Griffiths, M. (1995) *Feminisms and the Self: The Web of Identity* (London, Routledge).

Howe, K. R. (1997) *Understanding Equal Educational Opportunity: Social Justice, Democracy, and Schooling* (New York, Teachers College Press).

Macedo, S. (2000) *Diversity and Distrust: Civic Education in a Multicultural Democracy* (Cambridge, MA, Harvard University Press).

Olssen, M. (2001) Citizenship and Education: From Alfred Marshall to Iris Marion Young, *Educational Philosophy and Theory*, 33:1, pp. 77–94.

Sardoc, M. & Shaughnessy, M. (2001) An Interview with Iris Marion Young. *Educational Philosophy and Theory*, 33: 1, pp. 95–102.

Stone, Lynda (2000) Embodied Identity: Citizenship Education for American Girls, in: M. Arnot & J. A. Dillabough (eds), *Challenging Democracy: International Perspectives on Gender, Education and Citizenship* (London, RoutledgeFalmer).

Tamir, Y. (2003) Education and the Politics of Identity, in: R. Curren (ed.), *A Companion to the Philosophy of Education* (London, Blackwell) pp. 501–508.

Young, I. M. (1989) Polity and Group Difference: A Critique of the Ideal of Universal Citizenship, *Ethics*, 99: 2 pp. 250–274.

Young, I. M. (1990) *Justice and the Politics of Difference*, (Princeton, NJ, Princeton University Press).

Young, I. (2000) *Inclusion and Democracy* (Oxford, Oxford University Press).

# 1

# Education and the Politics of Difference: Iris Young and the politics of education

AVIGAIL EISENBERG
*University of Victoria*

The relation between education and democracy is a difficult one. Even the wealthiest countries with highly educated populations have failed to develop educational systems that provide adequate educational experiences and opportunities for individuals within all social groups. In Canada, for instance, an aboriginal youngster has a better chance of being sent to prison than completing university.[1] In the United States, a wide and alarming disparity exists between the educational achievement of minority students, in particular Hispanics and African Americans, and white students from grade 3 onwards.[2] These failures have led to debates about how to attain equal educational opportunity, how to understand the role educational systems play in sustaining or undermining racism and other forms of oppression, and how to identify the strategies available through educational systems to dismantle oppression and enhance the well-being of those who are members of socially disadvantaged groups.

At the centre of these debates are questions about the nature of equality, whether and how best to recognize diversity amongst social groups, and how to reconcile diversity and democratic participation. With these questions and issues in mind, I examine three key contributions that Iris Young has made to democratic political theory and the ways in which her contributions might play out in relation to education.[3] To be clear, Young has not directly applied her ideas to educational policy.[4] But attempts to think through of the problems encountered in the politics of education, especially the profound challenges mentioned above, lead to debates that are central to Young's projects.

First, Young has argued that oppression and domination, not distributive inequality, ought to guide discussions about justice. Therefore equalizing educational opportunities requires eliminating oppression, not merely developing a calculus by which to allocate resources equally. Second, eliminating oppression requires establishing a politics that welcomes difference by dismantling and reforming structures, processes, concepts and categories that sustain difference-blind, impartial, neutral, universal politics. Third, a politics of difference requires restructuring the division of labour and decision-making so as to include disadvantaged social groups but allow them to contribute without foregoing their particularities.

This essay also examines three challenges to Young's theory. The first challenge is whether a politics of difference, of the sort for which Young argues, is substantively distinct from a politics that focuses on redistributing wealth and if it is, then, second, whether or not it offers a normatively better approach to social justice. The third challenge is whether, by emphasizing differences amongst social groups, a politics of difference diverts resources from efforts to address material deprivation and undermines the social solidarity upon which redistributive politics relies. Does difference, and specifically Young's understanding of difference, lead to social fragmentation of the sort that jeopardizes social justice? The first two parts of the essay set out Young's theory and the general political strategies that follow from her theory. The third part examines some practical changes to educational institutions and practices entailed by a politics of difference. Finally, the fourth part examines three challenges to Young's approach and how they might play out in debates about structuring an educational system.

## I

According to Young, social justice requires dismantling structures of oppression and domination, and oppression and domination are not merely about how resources are distributed. This is not to say that disparities in wealth have nothing to do with unequal educational opportunity and achievement. Rather, the concern is that, as important as universal accessibility to education (or any other public good) is, it is not, by itself, enough to ensure that all individuals are treated justly by institutions or, in the case of education, that the system is doing its utmost to secure social justice. Unequal educational achievement and opportunity will persist in socially diverse societies even if schooling and educational programs are fully accessible to all students (Young, 1990, p. 26). This is because equalizing resources does not, by itself, address all the forms of injustice that have a direct impact on undercutting the opportunities and achievements of individuals within socially disadvantaged groups. In particular, universal accessibility and policies which seek to treat all individuals precisely the same, do not address the sources of many forms of oppression and domination that are directly experienced by groups in every society. Young identifies five 'faces of oppression' that are not reducible to one common source and are not alleviated by distributing resources equally. These are exploitation, marginalization, powerless, cultural imperialism and violence (Young, 1990, chp. 2).

The relation between distributive issues and oppression is complex. Some, though not all, forms of oppression tend to be implicated in distributive issues but none is merely a matter of distribution. In fact, some forms of oppression are not affected whatsoever by reforming the distributional pattern, while other forms are affected but not dismantled or transformed. For instance, the oppression experienced through cultural imperialism often intersects with the ways in which resources are distributed in the sense that imperialism has often entailed taking away the resources upon which an indigenous group thrives and thereby causing that group to experience material deprivation and alienation from its way of life over a long term. This, in turn, can have profound consequences in perpetuating social disadvantages for that group, including material disadvantages. But attempts to rectify imperialism by redistributing material resources or even by using affirmative action as a means to rebalance access to opportunities or compensate for the effects of historical injustice will not dismantle imperialism. At best, such measures will address some symptoms that arise because of imperialism. Neither redistribution, nor, in many cases, affirmative action in employment or education opportunities will correct the historical imbalance caused by colonialism if that imbalance continues to structure cultural, political, legal, and social symbols and institutions. This is because how resources are distributed is often the symptom of a problem whose sources lay with the structures and institutions through which distribution is managed. What counts as a resource in a particular society, whose abilities are prized and whose are devalued, to what extent the contributions of a group are recognized or ignored, utilized or marginalized, are matters central to determining how oppression and domination work. Sometimes these matters directly implicate how resources are distributed. But sometimes they do not.

Two further problems with distributive theories of justice are, first, that they provide a misleading account of the nature of social injustice by assuming that power is an alienable resource that can be traded, exchanged, and equalized. They assume that alienable resources can be taken from us, if we have too much of them, or given to us, if we don't have enough. Second, distributive approaches assume that the nature of power is such that it lies in the hands of particular people or agents (and can be taken away from them) and not in the hands of others. Agents, such as the ruler and the subject, the husband and the wife, the judge and the prisoner, are the models often used to discuss unequal distributions of power.

Together, these two assumptions work well when the task at hand is to understand injustice in terms of the distribution of resources amongst individuals; for instance, to compare the resources that some individuals enjoy, and to assess whether some people have more than others to devote to educational programs. But the logic does not work so well to reveal, for instance, the ways in which sexual exploitation, racism or marginalization work to distort the opportunities of most, though usually not all, individuals within particular social groups. This is because oppression is sustained by processes and structures, not merely particular agents or distributional patterns. Systems of domination such as patriarchy and imperialism, guide whole processes of social, political and economic interaction and through these processes influence how resources are distributed, how people are recognized by others, how agents gain and keep power and how power is withheld from others.

Another illustration of how the distributive paradigm is poorly designed to address oppression is the case of social violence. Violent acts that tend to target particular groups of people, such as gay bashing, racial and sexual harassment or assault, are a source of oppression that is non-distributive and that is sustained by processes and structures rather than particular agents. This is not to say that specific people don't commit these crimes. Rather, the point is that each act of violence may be carried out irrationally, in the sense that those responsible usually do not view themselves as coordinating a larger strategy of oppression. Nonetheless, the cumulative effect is that some types of violence are a source of oppression for particular groups of people and this is so even though most members of the group will never have experienced violence. Violence feeds into and informs the processes through which sexism, homophobia and racism are reinforced. Some forms of violence shape the identity of individuals who are members of targeted social groups, like women, gay men, and racial minorities. While resources might be used to protect groups more effectively from violence, the way in which violence is manifested goes far beyond what a conventional redistributive scheme can aspire to accomplish. Addressing the oppression to which some acts of violence contribute entails, in part, dismantling the social structures in which sexism, homophobia and racism fit and not merely increasing the policing and security in neighbourhoods, on campuses, and in schools.

By focusing on the presence of oppression rather than the unfair distribution of resources, we are forced to focus on a set of social problems that are far broader in scope, more deeply embedded in social relations than are the problems that are related to distribution. Oppression implicates not simply who has what, but also how people think about themselves and about others, how they act, what they desire and what symbols, structures and processes lead them to think and act the way that they do. As a result, addressing oppression, and therefore 'dismantling the social structures in which sexism, homophobia and racism fit' is an exceedingly tall order. Young admits that nothing short of a 'cultural revolution' (Young, 1990, p. 152) is required to rid society of oppression because oppression is sustained by so many social structures and processes in so many different ways.

The social relations that are important to sustaining oppression include the division of labour, decision-making power and procedures, and cultural forms of interacting and communicating. Addressing oppression requires that we take note of, first, how social groups are positioned in relation to each other, second which social groups enjoy non-material goods such as respect, power, and opportunity and, third, how the enjoyment of these goods is sustained by particular social relations (Young, 1990, p. 16). In doing so, what becomes exceedingly clear is that social inequality is structural in the sense that it is reproduced by social processes 'that tend to privilege some more than others'. (Young, 2001, p. 2). Unlike rules that either allow or bar all individuals within a particular category from engaging in a specified activity (e.g. 'No Blacks need apply'), social processes create tendencies, through incentives and disincentives that affect social groups without necessarily directing the behaviour of each and every individual. This reveals the ways in which oppression is group-based in the sense that it can be detected only by comparing the situations of social groups, not by comparing the situations of unsituated individuals. Any given individual might or might not find a way of negotiating the social processes to their advantage. The social inequality that characterizes a society is located in patterns of injustice that are reinforced by processes that treat some groups unjustly.

So, given that oppression is structural and group-based, the ways to address social inequality entail restructuring social institutions and processes so that they reflect, recognize and value the differences amongst social groups. Young's notion of a 'politics of difference' focuses on group-based differences and seeks to sever the link between difference and social disadvantage by treating difference as a political resource in the sense that group difference and its relation to social disadvantage becomes the focus of politics and political reform.

In sum, social justice ought to be viewed as the absence of oppression, not merely as the fair redistribution of resources. Oppression has (at least) five faces, according to Young, some of which intersect with redistributive issues, but some of which exist with or without problems associated with unfair distributive schemes. In addition to mistaking sources and symptoms of oppression, distributive theories tend to view power as alienable and are agent-focused. Both tendencies impede understanding how oppression can be dismantled. Dismantling oppression requires, minimally, understanding that what feeds and shapes oppression and domination including the structures, habits, institutions, and modes of discourse by which the faces of oppression are sustained and advanced. So, just as every institution and social structure is implicated in sustaining oppression, each is also implicated in dismantling it by recognizing, legitimizing and valuing group differences.

## II

Chief amongst the structural targets of a politics of difference is the liberal notion of impartiality and the ideals of neutrality, universalism and merit, each of which, Young argues, relies on impartiality. The liberal belief in the existence of an impartial point of view and of impartiality as a standard in moral reasoning has the consequence of eliminating from liberal reasoning the particularities of different perspectives including passion, emotion, personal knowledge and experience, and thus the real differences amongst people. Impartiality attempts to put aside difference and, in its place, construct standards and values that transcend differences. The impartial subject is able to reason or represent values in a manner that transcends differences amongst people. These transcendent values are central to how liberals conceive of the civic public (Young, 1990; chp. 4), citizenship (Young, 1989), and the democratic polity (Young, 2000). They inform what Young calls the 'myth of merit' (Young, 1990, chp. 7). In each case, the impartial values erase the particularities of all but the dominant group. The values of citizenship, of the public vs. private, and of what we consider merit to consist of are all presented as value-neutral, universal, and standardized, when they are not. These neutral, universal and impartial categories often carry with them implicit values to which not all social groups have full or equal access. Thus, they deny group difference. In part, the denial of group difference is what liberalism aims at in the sense that it aims to secure the fair and equal treatment of all individuals regardless of their differences. But this aim is easily distorted in ways that entrench the disadvantages suffered by some groups because of their historical, cultural, and/or economic relation to the dominant group.

A good example of this problem in education is when merit is assessed using standardized tests (Young, 1990, pp. 207–10). Standardized tests are often used as means to determine which students can vie for access to prestigious schools and programs. And these schools and programs then influence which individuals can vie for particular jobs. But many educators have pointed out that neither the tests nor applicant or job performance assessments are value-neutral or objective in terms of the cultural meanings they emphasize.[5] What this means precisely, is that assessments and evaluations which use particular cultural means and values as their standard, reconstitute differences amongst individuals as deviant or as having less value (Young, 1990, p. 209). This is not to suggest that all assessment is a bad idea. Rather, the point is that standards used in assessments are inevitably cultural and non-universal. If standardized tests and 'merit-driven' assessments are not free of cultural standards and values, and if making them impartial is impossible, then they do not provide an unbiased means of determining who gets access to privileged positions. But that is precisely how they are used. The unsurprising result of using them in this way is that the same hierarchies that inform social relations are reflected in which social groups get into the best schools and which ones have the best jobs.

Finally, impartiality also provides an ideological means of justifying non-democratic rule. If an impartial perspective is one that 'leaves behind particular affiliations, feelings, commitments and desires' (Young, 1990, p. 105), then decision-makers who are impartial, who have attained their jobs by excelling at 'neutral and merit-driven' assessment exercises, are ones that excel at adopting a 'universal' perspective which is 'neutral' amongst social groups in the sense that it is a perspective that putatively does not aim to validate the particular interests or values of a specific group. If our decision-makers adopt an impartial perspective, then we need not consult citizens or social groups affected by particular policies in order to figure out what is the best course to take. Thus, impartiality justifies non-democratic and hierarchical decision-making (Young, 1990, p. 111–6). The antidote to the ideological power of impartiality in all of its manifestations is to reformulate institutions so that they do not reduce differences and ignore particularities but rather aim at including differences by incorporating the particularities of social groups into decision-making. Essentially this entails instituting a system where an emphasis is placed on heterogeneity, on particularity, on accommodating and including group difference and on incorporating the perspectives of groups through group representation.

## III

Some heated political debates in the last 15 years revolve around the issue of whether political strategies that mobilize populations on the basis of ethnicity, gender, nationalism and other forms of identity-related differences have fractured progressive social movements and thereby undermined attempts to address the growing gap between the rich and poor. In political theory, Young has played a crucial role in these debates because, perhaps more than most theorists, her approach was developed at least initially by arguing that a politics of difference ought to replace a politics solely focused on distribution. In one sense, Young is surely correct that many issues and problems that are central to social injustice when it is conceived of as oppression are beyond the focus of debates about distributive justice. But few people view distributive justice as a magic elixir that eliminates all other forms of oppression. Analytically and practically, racism and sexism can exist with or without material deprivation. In most societies though, material inequality and cultural or racial oppression are intertwined. In fact, this is part of Young's point: as she puts it, 'the material effects of political economy are inextricably bound to culture' (Young, 1997, p. 148). The problem though, is whether emphasizing and recognizing the ways in which oppression and inequality manifest themselves separately, helps us to devise effective strategies that combat the different manifestations of injustice without playing one form of injustice off against the other. Has separating issues of difference from issues of distribution helped or hindered the cause of social justice?

This question is particularly relevant in education. Education is charged with the task of equalizing and expanding the opportunities of individuals both in terms of the jobs they might have access to and therefore the material resources they can hope to enjoy, and in terms of their role as citizens and therefore in terms of their cultural status, inclusion and political power. Given these tasks, educational institutions conventionally attempt to address what might be called 'non-distributive' forms of social disadvantage. For instance, educational curricula often include group-based 'consciousness raising' programs that promote racial awareness and awareness about date rape, that discourage bullying, that try to empower children so that they are less likely to be victims of assault by adults or that try to empower employees by making them aware of fair and unfair employment practices.

Such programs acknowledge one of Young's central messages, namely that resources are not themselves power without being sustained by structures and relations, such as a particular culture, an un/safe environment, an ex/in/clusive public, and a monopolization of information or knowledge, that give meaning, significance and thereby power to some resources or agents and not to others. Access to the best opportunities in society is denied to some groups not because explicit, discriminatory rules bar them from access (although this is still clearly a problem in some jurisdictions), nor only because they have less material resources to start with. Rather, the domination and oppression experienced by some individuals lead many to be denied dignity and respect, to have access only to poor choices, to be included only on terms that are alien to them, to exclude themselves, and to opt out. By focusing on difference and by critically discussing the ways in which some groups have more power than others and how this power works to exploit and oppress the vulnerable, consciousness raising programs try to turn differences that have been a source of disadvantage into a source of empowerment. Such programs help to illustrate the way in which 'opportunity has a wider scope than distribution' and that redistributing material resources may do nothing to dismantle social structures informed by racism, homophobia and sexism (to name only three examples).

While such programs might be consistent with Young's project, her approach is far more radical in several respects that give rise to concerns about conflicts amongst strategies. A politics of difference seeks to instantiate diversity 'all the way down' so to speak. For instance, while there are good reasons, from a democratic point of view, to oppose segregated schools, a politics of difference might legitimize limited forms of segregation or what Young calls 'differentiated solidarity', for the purpose of alleviating social disadvantage (Young, 2000, pp. 210–28) Separate schools or classes could be devoted to empowering a particularly disadvantaged group either by removing students from an environment dominated by the social habits and conventions by which their oppression is sustained (e.g. all-girls schools,

African American schools) or by focusing the curriculum on enabling a particular social group (e.g. Aboriginal people in Canada, the US, Australia and other states).

Yet, in most respects, the aim of a politics of difference is to create a heterogeneous public, not a segregated one. Young's conception of democracy is meant to be truly pluralistic. It relies on the ability of citizens to communicate with each other as equals from different social locations and perspectives. According to Young, 'we require real participatory structures in which actual people, with their geographical, ethnic, gender and occupational differences, assert their perspectives on social issues within institutions that encourage the representation of their distinct voices' (Young, 1990, p. 116). The best way to ensure that institutions and structures are sensitive to different perspectives and to the particularities of different social locations is to embrace democratic decision-making and participatory institutions that are difference-sensitive. A politics of difference requires institutions in which a politicized discussion about difference can take place and in which forums and media are available for alternative cultural experiment and play (Young, 1990, p. 152). In short, it requires a group-differentiated notion of citizenship and of social solidarity.

For example, in education, instituting difference would require an expanded social and educational understanding of literacy in the areas of history, art, music or literature so that the curriculum in these subject areas reflect the perspectives and values of different social groups. It would require reconfiguring how decisions are made within and about education by instituting a system of group representation in staffing decisions, school boards, and other public or political decision-making forums. Decision-making procedures and institutions that are sensitive to difference must ensure that the distinctive voices of disadvantaged social groups are articulated and heard. It would also require, within all institutions and decision-making forums, that discourse and communication was made sensitive to difference by considering the ways in which different groups communicate and present their reasons or justify their positions (Young, 2000, chp. 2). Dyadic argument is but one of many cultural forms (see Young, 2000, pp. 37–40). Difference-sensitive communication also creates a place for greeting, narrative, and rhetoric as means to convey and share the ideas and perspectives of different social groups (Young, 2000, pp. 57–77).

In all of these ways, a politics of difference requires the cultivation of an intellectual, political and social climate in which structures and institutions are sensitive to the differences amongst social groups and individuals. Contrary to liberal politics, wherein differences amongst individuals are 'officially' not used to determine one's status in decision-making, a politics of difference recognizes that social structures and institutions can only address oppression and domination by making space for difference and by not reducing difference to some impartial, neutral or universal perspective. Justice requires paying attention to the ways in which differences have structured social relations and then restructuring these relations accordingly.

## IV

For Young's critics, these more radical strategies are the ones that potentially undermine the redistribution of resources or equalization of opportunities. The concern is that, in the course of 'paying attention' to differences, far fewer resources and less attention is being paid to material deprivation. According to some critics, a politics of difference is fragmenting social movements and undermining social solidarity both of which are crucial to advancing causes of social justice. Three types of criticisms of Young's approach have been especially significant.

First, Young's approach has been criticized for emphasizing difference for differ-ence's sake, rather than viewing the recognition of difference as a means to alleviate the unfair distribution of resources and opportunities. Matters of distribution are not only central to social justice, according to critics such as Brian Barry. They exhaust concerns about social justice in the sense that unless an individual is deprived of resources or opportunities because of her so-called differences, there is no reason to suspect that she has suffered an injustice. There is no doubt, according to Barry, that 'the aspirations of group members tend to rise in line with the opportunities open to them' (Barry, 2001, p. 95). But Young's politics of difference putatively aims at ensuring, through group representation, that all groups participate proportionally in all walks of life regardless of whether their choices have been shaped by a denial of opportunities or resources. Whereas Barry argues that equality of opportunity in all walks of life is the key to social justice, he contends that it is a mistake to gage injustice merely in terms of the absence of a particular group in a particular occupation or in a particular decision-making role. In a just world, not all groups will be attracted to all jobs. Barry argues, for instance, that perhaps the reason why more women do not become corporate executives is because they have little inclination to have such a career. The absence of women in 'high-flying corporate executive' jobs might signal the need to investigate *whether* women are being unfairly denied opportunities. But their absence is not, in and of itself, evidence of unjust treatment. If opportunities and resources are equitably distributed (which Barry agrees, they are certainly not) an egalitarian liberal could not complain if women were underrepresented in some jobs (Barry, 2001, p. 94).

Barry's criticism, at best, reveals an ambiguity in Young's theory. On one hand, Young makes it clear and obvious throughout her work that the point of a politics of difference is to address social injustice and not to instantiate difference for the sake of difference (see especially, Young, 2000, pp. 92–9 and 102–8). Where she might part with Barry is on what counts as social injustice. Because her approach rests on scepticism about universality, neutrality, and 'the myth of merit', and because it raises a suspicion that these ideals contribute to group oppression, her analytical framework is especially sensitive to detecting ways in which difference is stifled. This means that the politics of difference does not merely scrutinize the opportunities open to people as they strive to attain credentials, to secure particu-lar jobs, or make careers for themselves. It also requires that credentials, jobs and careers are structured so as not to exclude difference and thereby exclude people who belong to disadvantaged social groups. It is not all that difficult to understand the way in which 'top corporate executive' jobs (to use Barry's example) are less welcoming of people who are the primary caregivers to small children or the elderly (usually women), or who aren't already part of a network of clubs and groups based on privilege (e.g. graduates of prestigious schools, members of exclusive sport clubs, etc.). Perhaps women 'just choose' not to contend for such jobs–but surely their choices are driven by the way in which particular jobs interact with their social position (see Young, 2001; also see Anderson, 1999).

Often the qualifications for a particular job, despite being standardized and merit-driven, privilege the characteristics of particular social groups. Or conversely, sometimes a set of characteristics typical of a particular social groups happen to be a liability within a particular job. Even where qualifications are standardized and competitions merit-driven, and even in cases where employers would be delighted to find amongst willing applicants a woman or member of a visible minority, positions can still be structured in unjust ways. If particular jobs cannot accommodate people who devote time to care-giving, or if they penalize minorities by relying, even informally, on social networks typically less accessible to those outside the white male mainstream, then they are likely to replicate the social injustice that characterizes the particular society in which they are situated.

Barry's position is surely mistaken if what it amounts to is a denial that members of minority communities can be marginalized in public institutions even if they are welcome to send their children to public schools, to compete for places in universities, to enter professions, and to run for political office. Despite impartial rules, institutional structures, standards and values resist group difference in a myriad of ways. Even without formal or financial barriers, these institutions can alienate individuals who come from communities which are significantly different from the majority. Institutions need to confront all the ways in which they potentially adhere to the values and standards of one dominant community. Therefore, a radical reorganization of educational institutions, including the curriculum, staffing, and decision-making processes, along lines that embed group-based difference in each aspect of the system, makes good sense if the project is to dismantle social disadvantage. Even uncontroversial programs, such as cultural or racial awareness education, are likely to be rendered impotent if they are at odds with the general thrust of the regular curriculum, if they are contradicted by how decision-making works in a school, how staffing decisions are made, or how students and teachers treat each other. If the content of the curriculum, the way in which students are assessed, the structure of the school day, or the treatment they receive from other students and teachers, neglects or is hostile to the values of all communities, except for one dominant one, it will hardly be surprising to find that children from minority groups will not perform as well as those within the majority.

But it is difficult to tell whether Barry would argue otherwise. Barry's criticisms of Young lose much of their strength in light of the fact that, as he notes, liberal societies are so far away from providing equal opportunities to their members that a radical departure from an individual choice or merit-based model, possibly along the lines that Young advocates, could be justified for the foreseeable future (Barry, 2001, p. 95). In other words, Barry might agree that group representation is valuable to rectify social injustice if it could be shown that, for instance, role models help to equalize opportunities. But, the important goal, according to Barry, is essentially a redistributive one, whereas, putatively, for Young, a politics of difference aims at equalizing the division of labour, the organization of decision-making and the status of cultural meaning (Young, 1997, p. 153) even if opportunities and resources are equal.

A second type of criticism of Young's approach focuses on the question of just how deeply different is a politics of difference.[6] Opening the doors to diversity in public institutions, especially educational institutions, and radically reorganizing them in terms of group difference, as Young's theory suggests, may pose serious challenges to developing a heterogeneous public. Again, Young's intentions are clearly not to embrace difference for difference's sake. Universality 'in the sense of the inclusion and participation of everyone in moral and social life' is precisely what her approach aims at creating (Young, 1990, p. 189). Further she argues that group difference is fluid and relational and therefore is not a 'natural' kind of thing that needs recognition just because it exists (Young, 2000, p. 87). Rather, it needs recognition when it is a source of oppression or when it intersects with and is used to entrench oppression. Recognition, esteem or respect of group difference is a means to emancipate particular groups which are caught in social relations that turn their identity, class, gender, or nationhood into a source of oppression.

Although Young is correct that a true sense of inclusion requires, not that groups abandon their particularity, but that their differences are included and accommodated in the public sphere, whether it is reasonable to include all groups in the public sphere depends in part on what sort of groups and what sort of group differences are viewed as the kind that need inclusion. While neutrality that disguises racial or cultural privilege is clearly unjustified, the question of religious difference and the secularism of public institutions pose more difficult examples. In relation to religion, which after all informs the values and perspectives of many social groups, opening the doors to diversity in public institutions, especially educational institutions, and radically reorganizing them in terms that value and accommodate group difference, might pose serious challenges to developing a heterogeneous yet inclusive public. A politics of religious differences might invite into the public arena debates about religious values that have historically proven to be seriously divisive.

Again, education provides salient examples. One of the most profound challenges in education centres on whether schools ought to adhere only to secular values, or whether they ought to accommodate religious values.[7] While many educators might agree with Young that education ought to aim at creating a critical social environment in which instruction and discussion focus, in part, on confronting 'cultural images of appropriate pursuits for girls and boys' or making visible, 'the achievements of women and people of colour' (Young, 1990, pp. 2, 6–7), certainly not all educators would agree and many would advance their disagreement on the basis of group difference. In the United States and Canada, for example, religious groups form powerful coalitions to actively resist exposing their children to a wide array of values, especially values about religious diversity, sexual equality, and sexual orientation. The central and motivating issues of several prominent court cases have been whether religious communities can shield their children from exposure to diversity as a means to protecting their religious difference. In the case of *Yoder v Wisconsin*, for instance, the Amish argued that removing their children from the educational system at the age of 14 to begin working in the community was a way of ensuring community survival by, amongst other things, minimizing the exposure of their children to the outside world.[8] In the *Mozert* case, Christian fundamentalists objected to a book partly because, amongst other things, it briefly portrayed a boy making toast for a girl and thus, according to the religious community, challenged the gender division of labour that they viewed as central to their distinctive way of life and endorsed by their holy book.[9]

Does Young's approach aim at accommodating religious difference? It is difficult to say and the question raises several challenging issues. The first challenge is whether a politics of difference provides any guidance for how to deal with insular minorities. On one hand, groups that insulate themselves from the mainstream undermine the goal of developing a heterogeneous public. On the other hand, some groups, like the Amish, survive partly on the basis of insulating themselves, and more significantly, insulating their children from social diversity and modernity.[10] A second and broader challenge is whether societies should allow separate schools for purposes other than alleviating social disadvantage. Liberal societies have often dealt with the need to respect religious freedom by allowing groups to institute separate schools in which the partial perspective of a particular religion can be used as the basis of education. But it is certainly not clear that a politics of difference would endorse this sort of solution because it is unclear whether separate religious schools help to build or undermine an inclusive and heterogeneous public (see Spinner-Halev, 2000, chp. 5).

Finally, although one could argue that religious groups, unlike racialized groups, are not subject to systematic social disadvantage based on difference, some religious minorities might defer and argue instead that religious groups suffer social disadvantage if they live in a secular society where religious difference is stifled in public institutions. Moreover, the liberal solution to religious diversity, namely toleration and rights which guarantee freedom of religion to all religious groups, is more difficult to defend if one eschews, as Young's approach does, a notion of liberal impartiality and neutrality. But it also seems difficult to reconcile social justice with a democratic order that extends group representation in all public institutions to religious groups and expands democratic discourse so that it includes religious reasons or at least religious ways of justifying reasons.

The third type of criticism of Young's approach focuses on the practical consequences of following a politics of difference rather than a politics that focuses on social solidarity across differences. Nancy Fraser argues that a politics of redistribution and a politics of recognition are weakening the political Left. Unlike Barry, Fraser agrees with Young that not all types of social injustice can be reduced to a politics of redistribution. Nonetheless, a politics of difference causes group identity to supplant class interest as the 'chief medium of political mobilization' and it leads to cultural recognition displacing socioeconomic redistribution 'as the remedy for injustice and the goal of political struggle' (Fraser, 1997a, p. 11). According to Fraser, this displacement occurs in both theory and practice. When groups mobilize to address issues of social injustice, they appear to be caught in an impossible contradiction between, on one hand, seeking to eliminate group-specific positions in the division of labour, and, on the other hand, seeking to affirm group identities and group representation of those identities in the divisions of labour. The alarming result is that, in order to retain or attain group solidarity, social movements will engage in massive mobilization efforts 'in which not a single socio-economic demand ... [is] raised' (Fraser, 1997b, p. 126).

This concern, that recognition issues have a way of distracting attention and diverting resources from redistribution issues, has been observed and reiterated in many different settings. For instance, associations, such as labour unions, that pursue broad agendas and rely on group solidarity to do so, can find themselves internally divided into subgroups, each of which seeks accommodation and privilege in order to have their group difference recognized (see Creese, 1999). Broader implications of this problem have been traced by a set of critics who argue that a radical form of multiculturalism, of the sort that Young endorses, undermines the social solidarity and trust upon which the welfare state relies (Miller, 1995, p. 135). 'Psychological studies of justice ... show', according to David Miller, 'that people are more likely to afford equal treatment to others with whom they share a common identity or common values' (Miller, 1998, p. 48). Group difference undermines this common identity and thereby jeopardizes solidarity and trust. Solidarity based on a shared identity cultivates trust and reciprocity of the sort upon which large-scale social welfare programmes rely (Miller, 1995, p. 139). Whereas a shared cultural or national identity facilitates this reciprocity, diversity and especially a politics that mobilizes individuals on the basis of their group differences undermine reciprocity and thus jeopardize the redistributive programs upon which reciprocity and trust rely. Public institutions, such as public education, that have been weakened by the diminishing public commitment to finance them, become even weaker in societies enamored of group difference.

Fraser may be correct, that a politics which focuses on group difference rather than how wealth is distributed poses serious strategic challenges to addressing material deprivation in a political context. This is partly because, unlike philosophical discussions, politics tends to be a zero-sum game. Activist groups must choose how to expend their resources and such choices make a difference to the types of injustice that are likely to be addressed by public institutions. So even if there is no theoretical obstacle to stop groups from fighting injustice on all fronts, the obstacles are substantial from a political and pragmatic point of view. Groups that focus on dismantling social structures, for instance, by lobbying for a process that privileges candidates from disadvantaged groups, are choosing not to protest against budget cuts to schools or particular programs (see Gitlin, 1995). Moreover, the obstacles to fighting injustice on all fronts are buttressed in political contexts where material redistribution is more publicly controversial than is, for example, teaching children tolerance and cultural sensitivity. Unsurprisingly, difficult issues of redistribution may be happily put aside by governments in favour of efforts to recognize the contributions of marginalized groups, for instance, by including culturally-sensitive materials in the school curriculum, by ensuring that classes are racially diverse, or by hiring a principal from a disadvantaged group.[11]

Of course, there is nothing new to the strategy of 'divide and conquer' and so the concern that Miller, Fraser, and even Barry raise may amount to nothing more than a cautionary tale that those who support a politics of difference should be aware of unintentionally playing into the hands of the cost-cutting agenda of neo-liberals and other foes of the welfare state. In this respect, consider the strange politics that has emerged in the 2003 US Supreme Court decision of *Grutter v Bollinger*.[12] In this case, the majority on the court upheld affirmative action programs at University of Michigan Law School partly on the basis that creating a diverse environment in the law school is an important and valuable goal–which it surely is. Although the Court's main reason seems to embrace a politics that recognizes the social disadvantages of the African American minority and takes seriously the need to ensure that African Americans have access to privileged institutions, the decision does little to draw into the question the legitimacy of privileged institutions in the first place. To the contrary, it seems to advance the commitment in American society to a politics of economic privilege as long as economic privilege is not race-based as well. One message of this case is that institutions of privilege, namely law schools and universities, ought not to be institutions of racial domination. This message was reflected in the *amicus curiae* submitted in this case. An unprecedented number of organizations and social groups across the political spectrum, including significantly, military officers, and Fortune 500 companies, urged the court to embrace diversity for the sake of a racially tolerant and culturally sensitive workforce and military.

On one hand, this case illustrates that, as Fraser points out, the political challenge of addressing social injustice of one sort without exacerbating injustice of another sort is at the heart of a politics of difference. Young's approach might offer a more subtle and accurate understanding of the plural nature of oppression, but in doing so it may inadvertently encourage a political division in reform strategies and this division may end up dividing and weakening efforts to combat social injustice.

On the other hand, it would be a mistake to suggest that Young's approach would condone *Grutter v Bollinger* since part of the aim of her approach is to dismantle privilege. It is also worth adding that empirical studies have found no evidence that the decline of the welfare state is connected to or exacerbated by the presence of policies which recognize and accommodate group-based differences, such as multiculturalism.[13] To the contrary, there are good reasons to suppose that improving the accommodation of marginalized groups will increase the extent to which these groups view themselves as part of a heterogeneous public and therefore as activist participants in societal decision-making. In the end, this third challenge may be based more on conjecture than on fact.

## V

The relation between education and democracy is a difficult one partly because of how important education is to the realization of equality of opportunity and to developing the abilities and thus empowering individuals across all groups in society. A politics of difference aims at taking political reform well beyond questions of how best to allocate material resources. How resources are allocated is important to be sure. But reallocation might do little to address the structural barriers that sustain disadvantage. Similarly, the underachievement of social groups in education needs to be addressed in part by finding and dismantling the social structures that sustain oppression. Although Young does not outline how this is done in education, one assumes that her strategies would include, minimally, curricula that reflect the multicultural, multinational, and multilingual nature of society, programmes that raise awareness of how racism, sexism and homophobia manifest themselves, decision making structures that ensure that the voices of parents, teachers and community leaders from disadvantaged groups are affirmatively incorporated. Schools should hire teachers and principals from disadvantaged social groups and parent committees and school boards must include representatives from these groups. The point of these changes is to address forms of injustice that are not merely a matter of redistributing resources, and to do so in a way that reflects that oppression is often not agent dependent but rather sustained by larger structures and institutions. Oppression is aimed at social groups. Individuals who act as agents for oppression are sometimes simply doing their job, or applying standards which seem, on their face, value neutral and impartial. To address oppression requires mobilizing social groups, providing them with arenas of communication in which they can best expose and reformulate structures that deny or devalue their group difference.

The critics have posed three types of challenges to Young's theory. First, difference might be merely another way of getting at inequality of resources or opportunities, and if it is not, then, second, a politics of difference might value difference for difference's sake rather than for the sake of alleviating social disadvantage. Here I have suggested that, although Young's theory is clear focused on alleviated social disadvantage, some examples of difference, such as religious difference, pose difficult challenges to her approach. It is difficult to imagine that democracy would be better off viewing secularism as a form of false neutrality and instead including religious values in forums of democratic deliberation and decision-making. At the same time as religious difference is a challenge to Young's approach, it is precisely the sort of challenge that leads us to think critically about social injustice beyond the confines of distributive approaches, about what ought to count as social disadvantage and about what causes people to be included and excluded in public institutions–all of which are firmly within Young's agenda.

The third challenge is whether a politics that focuses on difference diverts social resources from a politics focused on redistribution and fragments social solidarity. To be sure, focusing on one form of injustice is bound to cause conflict with those who have different priorities. These are difficult conflicts, but perhaps they are precisely the sort that need to be confronted in order to advance social justice. Moreover, even if a politics focused on group difference had the effect of undermining social solidarity, the way to understand this problem would turn crucially on why the focus on group difference putatively has this effect. It could be, as the critics suppose, that social solidarity is jeopardized when public attention focuses on what distinguishes rather than what unites people. But the problem could also arise because group difference draws into question the dominance of a particular social group and therefore diminishes the motivation of that dominant group to set the terms of participation and of the agenda pursued. This latter problem certainly poses challenges to progressive social movements. And while these challenges are beyond the scope of this paper, the problem is not to be solved by giving up on group difference.

## Notes

1. Canadian Human Rights Commission, quoted in Turtle Island Native Network–Education http://www.turtleisland.org/front/_front.htm
2. For a detailed assessment of black-white disparities in the US, see Jacobson, *et al.*, 2001.
3. See also Howe 1997, esp. chp. 4. Howe applies the ideas of several political theorists, including Young, Susan Okin, Amy Gutmann, Carol Gilligan and others, to the question of how educational equality might be attained.
4. Young discusses her work in relation to education in an interview conducted by Mitja Sardoc and Michael F. Shaughnessy, 2001.
5. In addition to the numerous studies cited by Young (1990: 206–10), there are many organizations which lobby against standardized tests because of their biases. In the US, The National Association for Fair and Open Testing, and in Canada, the Canadian Teacher's Federation are two such organizations, both of which have published several studies outlining the biases endemic to such tests.
6. For a detailed examination of this question, along more philosophical lines, see Trebble 2002.
7. For an excellent discussion of this problem see Spinner-Halev, 2000.
8. *Wisconsin v Yoder*, 406 US 208 (1972). Also see discussion of Yoder in Macleod, 1997.
9. *Mozert v Hawkins* 827 F2d 1058 (6th Cir 1987). Also see discussion in Spinner-Halev 2000 pp. 112–5.
10. Children raise some of the most challenging problems in such examples. For an exploration of these themes see Archard and Macleod eds 2001.
11. See, for example, Goulbourne's discussion of Britain's Swann Report on educational reform. Goulbourne 1991, esp. 221.
12. *Grutter v Bollinger* (288 F3d 732) SC 2003.
13. For an interesting study on this topic, see Banting and Kymlicka 2003.

## References

Archard, D. & C. Macleod (eds) (2001) *The Moral and Political Status of Children* (Oxford, Oxford University Press).

Banting, K. & W. Kymlicka (2003) Do Multiculturalism Policies Erode the Welfare State? Paper presented to the Colloquium Francqui 2003, *Cultural Diversities versus Economic Solidarity*, Brussels.

Barry, B. (2001) *Culture and Equality* (Cambridge, MA, Harvard University Press).

Creese, G. (1999) *Contracting Masculinity: Gender, Class, and Race in a White-Collar Union, 1944–1994* (Toronto, Oxford University Press).

Fraser, N. (1997a) *Justice Interruptus: Critical Reflections on the 'Postsocialist' Condition* (New York, Routledge).

Fraser, N. (1997b) A Rejoinder to Iris Young, *New Left Review*, 223, pp. 126–9.

Gitlin, T. (1995) *The Twilight of Common Dreams: Why America is Wrecked by Cultural Wars* (New York, Henry Holt).

Goulbourne, H. (1991) Varieties of pluralism: the notion of a pluralist post-imperial Britain, *New Community*, 17: 2.

Howe, K. (1997) *Understanding Educational Opportunity* (New York and London, Teacher's College Press).

Jacobson, J., C. Olsen, J. King Rice, S. Sweetland, and J. Ralph (2001) Educational Achievement and Black-White Inequality, *Educational Statistics Quarterly*, 3: 3.

Macleod, C. (1997) Conceptions of Parental Autonomy, *Politics and Society* 25: 1.

Miller, D. (1995) *On Nationality*. (Oxford, Clarendon).

Miller, D. (1998) The Left, the Nation-State, and European Citizenship, *Dissent*, 48: 47–51.

Sardoc, M. and M. F. Shaughnessy (2001) An Interview with Iris Marion Young, *Educational Philosophy and Theory*, 33: 1.

Spinner-Halev, J . (2000) *Surviving Diversity: Religion and Democratic Citizenship* (Baltimore and London, Johns Hopkins University Press).

Trebble, A. J. (2002) What is the Politics of Difference? *Political Theory* 30: 2.

Young, I. (1989) Polity and Group Difference: A Critique of the Ideal of Universal Citizenship, *Ethics*, 99 (January).

Young, I. (1990) *Justice and the Politics of Difference* (Princeton, NJ, Princeton University Press).

Young, I. (1997) Unruly Categories: A Critique of Nancy Fraser's Dual Systems Theory, *New Left Review*, 222, pp. 147–60.

Young, I. (2000) *Inclusion and Democracy*. (Oxford, Oxford University Press).

Young, I. (2001) Equality of Whom? Social Groups and Judgments of Injustice, *The Journal of Political Philosophy*, 9: 1.

## 2

# Multiculturalism and Citizenship: A critical response to Iris Marion Young

RONALD BEINER
*University of Toronto*

> What is a Left without a commons, even a hypothetical one? If there is no people, but only peoples, there is no Left.
> —Todd Gitlin, 1996, p. 165

Citizenship consists in sharing a political community, and enjoying the benefits and assuming the political responsibilities that give effect to this experience of shared political community. The challenge faced by contemporary multiculturalism is whether it can revise civic norms and practices in the way that its proponents desire without thereby undermining this core meaning of the idea of citizenship. Critical engagement with the work of Iris Marion Young can certainly help to clarify whether the politics of multiculturalism can meet this challenge.

In this essay, I will be focusing on Young's forceful argument in *Polity and Group Difference* because it offers the most theoretically radical statement of her civic vision, and also because it had an important impact on subsequent debates about multiculturalism and citizenship (Young, 1995, pp. 175–207).[1] Young starts her argument by acknowledging the moral grandeur of the original liberal-bourgeois ideal of citizenship articulated by the French Revolution: 'Citizenship for everyone, and everyone the same qua citizen' (p. 175). Without question, the ideal that animated this vision of citizenship was one of great moral power: equality of status 'as peers in the political public' (ibid.). But Young claims that by the late twentieth century, we have come to see that this liberal-egalitarian understanding of citizenship has not redeemed its promise. Even with the winning of full citizenship status (equal political and civil rights), important groups remain oppressed and excluded, reduced to second-class citizenship, and denied social justice (p. 176). 'Inclusion and participation ... in full citizenship' remains the goal, but '*differentiated* citizenship' now presents itself as a better route to that goal than 'equal treatment for all groups' (ibid.). The problem isn't just that an attractive normative vision turns out to be incapable of full realization. Young wants to argue that there are problems with the attractiveness of the normative vision itself. The fact that the liberal vision of universal citizenship didn't eventuate in full social justice for all the groups in the political community gave the disadvantaged groups a clearer insight into decisive flaws in the vision itself: a privileging of the notion of citizenship as 'having a common life with ... other citizens', at the expense of what ought to be a deeper affirmation of difference. Contemporary social movements, she thinks, have disclosed a superior civic vision: 'a positivity and pride in group specificity against ideals of assimilation' (ibid.). The term 'assimilation' obviously conjures up images of domination and coerced uniformity, so this suggests that if the universalist civic vision is associated with an assimilative ideal, it inevitably leads to oppression and enforced homogenization of cultural difference. What Young sees expressed in a regime of uniform citizenship is a politics of the general will that involves exclusion and enforcement of homogeneity. In response, she recommends a dual counter-vision: a radically transformed civic regime incorporating ambitious 'mechanisms for group representation'; and the replacement of equal treatment by 'special rights that attend to group differences' (p. 177).

In her discussion of 'citizenship as generality', Young focuses on contemporary theorists such as Benjamin Barber who aim to challenge existing civic practices by drawing upon the tradition of civic republicanism, and she criticizes these theorists for cleaving to an outmoded and in many ways pernicious Rousseauian image of political life.

> The ideal of the public realm of citizenship as expressing a general will, a
> point of view and interest that citizens have in common and that transcends
> their differences, has operated in fact as a demand for homogeneity among
> citizens (p. 178).

For Young, Rousseau's sexism is merely one indication of a much broader tendency in his political thought to enforce homogeneity among those who are included and exclude those (such as women) who represent heterogeneity. Here, I must confess, it seems to me unfair to try to discredit the politics of shared citizenship by bashing Rousseau. It's true that Barber and others appeal to Rousseau in some sense as an exemplary theorist of citizenship. But in fact Rousseau did not mean his construction of a republican utopia to be 'relevant' to the dilemmas of the contemporary state. The modern state is what he largely rejected, and he sketched a 'neo-ancient' (the ultimate oxymoron!) vision of political community precisely in order to highlight the deficiencies—or to get us to reflect more critically on the limits—of everything we associate with modern political norms and modern civic practices. When Rousseau rebuked modern citizens for substituting payment of taxes for the performance of public *corvées* (*Social Contract*, Book 3, chapter 15), this wasn't a 'proposal' for a restructuring of the modern state but rather an analysis of why the modern state as such couldn't be otherwise, with respect to essentials, than it appears in his critical characterization of its basic norms and institutions. The same applies to the question of cultural homogeneity versus cultural heterogeneity within the modern state: no modern state could possibly come close to meeting Rousseau's standards for a unitary civic identity, and Rousseau not only knows this, it's one of his main purposes as a theorist to display it as a compelling sociological reality.[2] The rejection of Rousseau's political thought as a model for contemporary reflection on civic unity surely doesn't suffice either as a proof that appeal to the idea of common citizenship necessarily requires 'that all citizens be the same' (p. 180), or as ruling out other (less extreme) models of a robust sharing of a common public realm.[3]

Young steadfastly rejects Barber's idea that there can be a 'common ordering of individual needs and wants into a single vision of the future in which all can share' (p. 182, quoting Barber, 1984, p. 224). A crucial part of what she sees as missing in this understanding of citizenship is its failure to come to terms with the necessary mediation of individual purposes by group membership. If we were essentially individuals, perhaps Barber's vision of citizenship would be viable. But since we are essentially members of groups (that is, groups less encompassing than the civic community itself), it is not viable. Rather, we are bound to horizons of experience and interest that are crucially shaped by our group membership. She calls this 'situated experience' (p. 183), and it clearly sets an important limit to how much we will be able to relate to or even understand fellow citizens who belong to other groups (p. 184: 'persons from one perspective or history can never completely understand and adopt the point of view of those with other group-based perspectives and histories'). This doctrine more or less ensures that there will always be something phony about the very notion of a citizen identity as such. Although Young wants to insist that there is no 'essentialism' in her view of group difference (p. 187), the idea that group perspectives are necessarily untranscendable does seem to point in the direction of essentialism.

In her second and third sections, on 'differentiated citizenship as group representation' and 'universal rights and special rights', Young lays out the substance of her alternative civic vision. The idea of group representation is a natural entailment of the ideas just discussed. If people can never hope to transcend their group-specific experience and are therefore bound to the horizons delimited by the history and perspectives of the group, then the only sensible way to empower them politically is by empowering the groups with which they identify. One political device that Young welcomes in this context is the idea of minority group vetoes (p. 189), which would certainly empower these groups *vis-à-vis* the rest of the political community but would not necessarily produce good outcomes and would definitely undermine the integrity of the political community as a whole as a site for legitimate decision-making on behalf of the totality of its citizens.[4] In fact, if such veto power were accorded to all the social groups that Young regards as oppressed, one could not envision a result other than general political paralysis, for in the case of each policy enacted by the polity, there is sure to be some group that will see its interests injured by its enactment. (Politics in Israel offers a good intimation of the systemic consequences of a *de facto* institutionalization of minority vetoes.)[5]

As for the more general project to ensure 'representation and recognition of the distinct voices and perspectives of' oppressed or disadvantaged groups (p. 189), there is some fluctuation in Young's argument as to whether it will move in a civic or anti-civic direction. First we get the weaker (more civic) rendering of the argument. According to this version of Young's argument, group representation is necessary because it is the only possible antidote to people's natural tendency to see the world only through the prism of their own interests:

> unless confronted with different perspectives on social relations and events, different values and language, most people tend to assert their own perspective as universal. (p. 190)

Hence the hardships of a disadvantaged group are opaque to a privileged group except insofar as the former are empowered to speak for themselves in the public realm. Yet there is something of a tension in the argument here: it seems to suggest a possibility of inter-group understanding, but Young wants very much to hold on simultaneously to the thesis of inter-group opacity. Young is insistent that however much trading of perspectives between groups may go on thanks to a propitious structuring of political institutions, there is never a real transcendence from group perspectives to a universal or general perspective: 'A general perspective does not exist' (p. 190); all relevant perspectives are untranscendable group perspectives. Still, Young allows herself to speak of group representation as an 'antidote' (or at least partial antidote) to 'circumstances of social oppression and domination' (p. 191). Within limits, even members of privileged classes can enlarge their perspectives somewhat if the structuring of political life guarantees an institutionalized voice to disadvantaged groups.

> As a person of social privilege, I am not likely to go outside of myself and have a regard for social justice unless I am forced to listen to the voice of those my privilege tends to silence. (p. 191)

Does Young herself, as a privileged person, need a report from a homeless person on the miseries of homelessness to know that this is a problem that society urgently needs to address? Isn't it often the case that those who work effectively on the political needs of the disadvantaged are themselves middle class rather than members of a disadvantaged group? In any case, the argument here is that a guaranteed political voice for disadvantaged groups will help those who are not disadvantaged to understand points of view that flow from things they have not experienced.

All of this constitutes a gesture acknowledging the possibility of mutual understanding between groups. But Young's deeper theoretical standpoint is that groups fundamentally *don't* understand each other, and that is why the basic political institutions of society need to be reconstituted so that people are recognized *as* members of groups and not *as citizens*. Young doesn't merely want guarantees of improved representation for blacks and women. Rather, she wants a thoroughgoing institutionalization of group representation that would remake political life from top to bottom (p. 193). She more or less concedes that it is not easy to picture what this new constitution would look like in detail; nonetheless, she thinks it can be done if people are convinced that her civic vision is the right one (ibid.).[6] Indeed, Young carries her group representation idea so far that some aspects of her vision of a 'heterogeneous public' give one the impression that the polity as a space of general deliberation virtually drops away altogether.[7] Seen in its most transformative aspect, this vision of a radically group-based politics makes it seem as if the only *real* public under this new dispensation would be the one that binds us together with those who share our group identity (for women: other women; for blacks: other blacks; for gays: other gays; and so on).[8] Telling in this regard is Young's interesting contrast between *traditional coalitions,* in which 'diverse groups work together for ends which they agree interest or affect them all in a similar way', and *rainbow coalitions,* in which different constituent groups pursue parallel goals while each of them 'affirms the specificity of its experience and perspective'—that is, each group expresses solidarity for other equally disadvantaged groups, but never loses sight of its ultimate allegiance to its own constituency (p. 192).[9] This may or may not be an effective political strategy in a society that is already deeply imprinted with group pluralism, but one should at least recognize that it involves forgoing an important dimension of common civic membership.

There is a second prong to Young's assault upon the idea of universal citizenship. Up until the point at which all groups were elevated to equal citizenship status, it made sense for emancipatory movements to set as their goal the achievement of equal citizenship. But now that the goal of equal rights for all groups has largely been met, the focus switches from equal rights to special rights for the disadvantaged. Despite important victories in the arena of liberal rights, 'group inequalities nevertheless remain', and hence a new conception of rights must be formulated that supersedes the liberal conception (p.196). Several of the issues that Young considers in this context are less controversial than she presents them as being: for instance, special arrangements for working women before and after childbirth, and special entitlements for disabled people. Many of the theoretically more complex issues have been addressed by other figures in the subsequent multiculturalism debates.[10] But what's interesting about Young's account is her argument that the point of group-differentiated rights is not just to allow disadvantaged groups to compete more effectively for desirable jobs and material rewards but to challenge the society's assumptions about what is *worth* rewarding—or, even more radically, to contest the notion that there should be privileged cultural norms at all. As Young puts it, the goal should be 'to denormalize the way institutions formulate their rules', rather than simply bend the rules to allow the disadvantaged to conform more easily to existing structures of social and political participation (p. 202; cf. p. 207, n. 20). One wonders what a fully 'denormalized' social world would look like; but the point that's worth emphasizing here is that Young isn't interested in a post-liberal regime of group-tailored rights merely in order to facilitate access on the part of various groups to social norms and opportunities as they currently exist.

In Young's vision of a transformed politics, there is 'publicly institutionalized self-organization' among disadvantaged groups (p. 193), more intensely democratized processes of public decision-making at the level of, for instance, neighborhood or district assemblies (p. 194), but also group assemblies to crystallize the group's position on a particular issue and choose its appointed representatives (ibid.), as well as group-based voting within a whole range of 'democratized workplaces and government decision-making bodies' (p. 193). In each of these arenas of intensified political agency, groups that Young designates as oppressed minorities would receive privileged political status, and, one presumes, non-oppressed groups would suffer diminished political status. The objections to Young's overall project are very familiar ones. I don't believe I have any new critical points to offer here, beyond the ones that have already been advanced by many critics. Let me just mention three standard criticisms:

1. Young is not interested in cultural minorities *per se*. Rather, she is interested in oppressed cultural minorities (or even in oppressed minorities where it is not obvious how to specify possession of a distinctive culture). What counts as being oppressed here, and what therefore qualifies a group as being a candidate for the special political prerogatives that Young favors?[11] As other critics have forcefully pointed out, members of oppressed groups as reckoned by Young far outnumber those not eligible for special political prerogatives, to the extent that members of the supposed 'dominant majority group' may themselves begin to feel that they constitute an embattled minority![12]

2. As Kymlicka and Norman point out, the fear on the part of Young's critics that her conception of differentiated citizenship 'would create a "politics of grievance"' is a reasonable worry: 'If, as Young implies, only oppressed groups are entitled to differentiated citizenship, this may encourage group leaders to devote their political energy to establishing a perception of disadvantage—rather than working to overcome it—in order to secure their claim to group rights'.[13]

3. Egalitarian politics requires solidarity and coalition-building. To the extent that each disadvantaged group focuses on 'pride in group specificity', it is less likely to sustain the kind of concern with *shared* problems and objectives required for a vibrant left-wing politics.[14] Clearly, this is the type of concern expressed in the epigraph from Todd Gitlin at the head of this article: if each ethnic and cultural community within the state comes to regard itself as a kind of quasi-polity of its own, and gives priority to securing its own sectional interests, one will have little reason to expect the political community to pull together in pursuit of social justice and the other goods of a shared political life. Such a view would have been axiomatic for earlier generations of the left, yet somehow the politics of cultural pluralism has come to seem more progressive than a politics of commonality.[15] Young, of course, can respond to this criticism by pointing to examples of 'rainbow coalition' politics (see pp. 192–193 and p. 206, n. 17). But it is at least arguable that the political left is likely to be more effective when it organizes its constituencies under a common banner, when it chooses as its preferred vehicle political parties and political movements that emphasize a common citizen identity.

Thus far, the discussion of group specificity has been fairly abstract. Let's see how Young's concept of group-differentiated citizenship plays out with respect to particular conflicts or potential conflicts between multiculturalism and citizenship. In the case of groups such as the Amish and Hasidic Jews in the United States, it seems a hopeless project to reconcile their culture with general citizenship; respecting their culture in these cases means tolerating their incapacity for citizenship.[16] We could only hope to turn them into good citizens by forcing them out of their cultures, and this doesn't seem an especially attractive policy.[17] (And Will Kymlicka and Wayne Norman are probably right that any project that seeks to fully incorporate Canadian and American aboriginal nations in a regime of common citizenship is also doomed to failure [Kymlicka & Norman, 1995, p. 308]).[18] In the case of what Kymlicka calls 'societal cultures' (i.e., *national* minorities), giving these national groups autonomous powers in regard to language, culture, education, immigration, and so on may offer the best chance of sustaining their commitment to a shared civic community (although as the Canadian experience shows, doing this even on a fairly expansive basis is no guarantee of success in the face of secessionist ambitions). But in the case of other minority cultures, their cultural membership is no reason for us to lower our expectations of their capacity for civic identity and civic membership. Any rendering of multiculturalist politics that seems to require an attenuation of shared citizenship gives us a reason to be wary of that version of multiculturalism rather than a reason to scale back on the claims of citizenship. To be sure, there are always disadvantages suffered by this or that minority in need of being remedied, such as political-legal remedies to discrimination suffered by homosexuals; but in principle, all these minorities should have the opportunity, and should fulfil this opportunity, to take up a full place in the civic order that enables its citizens to 'think of themselves as contributing to a common discourse about their shared institutions' (Barry, 2001, p. 301).

As regards Young's idea of differentiated political rights, there may well be good reasons in particular cases to grant special exemptions (or perhaps even special powers) to cultural minorities. In certain cases, at least, the exemptions needn't undermine the core understanding of citizenship shared by the whole society, which is a crucial consideration, since indeed they ought not to undermine that core understanding. Will Kymlicka and Wayne Norman, for instance, discuss how Sikhs in the Royal Canadian Mounted Police can be allowed to wear headgear different from what is mandated for other cultural groups without ill effects upon norms of civic equality.[19] This special right certainly doesn't do damage to the practice of citizenship; on the contrary, part of the rationale for the special right as Kymlicka presents it is precisely to enhance civic attachment on the part of the Sikhs.[19] But special exemptions for cultural groups do not always have either good or neutral consequences for citizenship; for instance, it can be plausibly argued that exemptions from military service for ultra-orthodox Jews in Israel do indeed undermine the core meaning of citizenship in that society. There is an agonizing debate in Israel today concerning this issue, and rightly so. The simple fact that a cultural minority *is* a minority facing special challenges in reproducing its way of life (which is the situation of Hasidic Jews in Israel) does not automatically entitle its members to be exempt from the responsibilities that other citizens bear in sustaining a regime of common citizenship.[20] And the awareness that sometimes such special rights will bolster citizenship, sometimes they will do the opposite, should make us quite cautious about allowing differentiated rights rather than encourage us to make the pursuit of such rights the foundation of a general political program. Conversely, a wholesale endorsement of multiculturalist politics will get in the way of a careful discrimination between accommodations of group demands that strengthen shared citizenship and those that weaken it.

Even if one concludes in the end that Iris Young's political prescriptions are unpersuasive, I think one needs to acknowledge that they offer an interesting and provocative alternative vision of what citizenship might look like in modern societies that are governed by tremendous social and cultural diversity. But ultimately, Young's civic vision is grounded in a deeper set of philosophical commitments—namely, a pervasive scepticism about what human beings *qua* human beings share, and whether universal categories of moral and political judgment can be brought to bear upon human affairs without self-mystification—and hence one's ultimate judgment of her political philosophy must be situated at this deeper philosophical level. Here, her verdict on Rousseau's political universalism—that it masks what is really just a parochially patriarchalist ideal (p. 179)—applies much more widely, and indicates a more general repudiation of universals.[21]

I think two points need to be made in response to this underlying stratum of Young's theoretical enterprise. First, it's not fully clear that the idea of inclusion (which remains a crucial moral goal for Young) retains its coherence if, according to the politics of difference, it's appropriate to jettison the interest in 'having a common life ... with other citizens' (p. 176). Inclusion only makes sense by reference to the shared political community in which the excluded aspire to be included. If this political community isn't really genuinely shared at all, inclusion seems like the wrong concept to capture the sort of moral-political aspiration at work here. Secondly, one suspects that in 'deconstructing' universalist moral and political categories, Young, like many other contemporary theorists influenced by post-modernism, is pulling the rug out from under her own political theory. (This point is somewhat related to the previous one.)[22] The rejection of moral universalism is clearly a moral and philosophical dead-end, for if there are no moral universals, then one cannot appeal to equality or justice, and if there is no possibility of appealing to these universals, then multiculturalism itself makes no sense.

Since this symposium issue is devoted to the relevance of Iris Young's work for education, I'll conclude this essay with some thoughts on this topic. In particular, I'll focus on a very instructive set of exchanges on the problem of education and citizenship in an interview with Michael Walzer conducted by Michael F. Shaughnessy and Mitja Sardoč. The lesson I draw from the crucial exchanges in this interview is that thinking about education in categories informed by a political theory like Iris Young's will tend to undermine the legitimacy of what would otherwise be essential educational goals: encouraging a shared civic identity and promoting sound practices of shared citizenship.

> [Shaughnessy/Sardoč:] Have racism, sexism, homophobia and other oppressive practices that stigmatize the groups outside of the political and cultural mainstream been exiled from the mainstream schooling with the acclaimed pluralism of the politics of recognition?
>
> [Walzer:] This is a loaded question. I suppose the answer is supposed to be no. But I am a little, maybe more than a little, skeptical about the oppression supposedly going on in our public schools—I mean, compared to real oppression in tyrannical states or totalizing religious communities. ...
>
> [Shaughnessy/Sardoč:] What do you think is the difference between 'inclusion'—the integration of previously marginalized groups—and 'assimilation'? How do these two differ in terms of educational policy?

[Walzer:] They might be the same thing, at least in one critical area. When we include members of minority groups as citizens, we also want to assimilate them to a single democratic political culture, and civics and history courses should be planned with that aim in mind. ...

[Shaughnessy/Sardoč:] How should we decenter the apparently universal values by the traditionally privileged cultural groups inscribed in the ruling stereotypes and prejudices which function as an invisible normative criteri[on]?

[Walzer:] Schools should teach universal values, front and center: the value of life, respect for other people, everyday kindness, democratic rights, and so on. (Shaughnessy and Sardoč, 2002, pp. 68, 70.)

What interests me in these exchanges is not so much Walzer's thoughtful answers but the ideological character of the questions that are put to him, and what they entail for the concept of citizenship. As Walzer remarks, they are loaded questions. All three of the questions I've quoted are implicitly anti-civic, and Walzer resists his questioners' drift because he clearly detects their anti-civic implication.

What we have here on the part of the interviewers is an ideological perspective that wants to see oppression, that wants to see hegemonic majorities trampling over excluded and marginalized minorities, and that as a matter of automatic reflex refuses to accept the notion that an appeal to universalistic conceptions could ever be anything other than a cover for particularistic hegemony. This is not to say, of course, that any society—even liberal societies at their best—ever achieves full justice in the relationship between dominant majorities and weaker minorities. Increasing the civic status of the latter is always an enrichment of citizenship for everyone, and there are always material preconditions for increasing the equality of civic status among the different groups within a society. But those who embrace the ideology of cultural oppression need to reflect more carefully on the price one pays when one rejects universalism (and thereby disparages citizenship). If the idea of the citizen *per se* is necessarily reducible to oppressed minorities on the one hand and oppressing majorities on the other hand, then the notion of *sharing* a political community makes no sense. And if the vision of a political community that is the political community of all its citizens is not a meaningful one, then in turn the conception of civic inclusion is rendered incoherent. To repeat a point we made in our critical response to Young, the idea of inclusion requires precisely a meaningful conception of what it is for all citizens to share a political community—implying a 'conception of politics as a society-wide conversation about questions of common concern' (Barry, 2001, p. 302).[23]

As Walzer discusses in response to another of Shaughnessy and Sardoč's questions, the building-up of a common community of citizens is a legitimate educational purpose of liberal societies. Even in cases, such as that of aboriginal nations or of fundamentalist religious groups, where the reproduction of a culture may seem to be an all-or-nothing affair and where we may sympathize with what minority cultures are up against in trying to keep their ways of life going in the face of a majority culture that is so radically different, still, we have to hold to an undiminished recognition of the legitimate claims of common citizenship:

[Members of these minority cultures claim] that they need total control over the education of their children. ... And then we, the democrats, come and say to them: But your children are going to grow up to be citizens; they are going to vote in our elections, and so we have an interest in making sure that they learn about democratic ways. ... [However understandable is the anxiety on the part of such minorities about reproduction of their culture,] the claims of citizenship are also very strong. In fact, these children don't belong only to their parents, they are also, so to speak, children of the republic. So we can insist that they learn something about the history and common values of the republic.[24]

The rhetoric of anti-universalism gets in the way of appreciating these unexceptional and unexceptionable purposes of democratic citizenship. As Russell Jacoby has sensibly pointed out, there is inevitably a price to be paid for the renunciation of universalism, including civic universalism:

A preference for the local and the specific is benign, even salutary. What is wrong with favoring the unique and distrusting universals? In the short run, nothing. Yet over time the suspicion of universals takes its revenge. Despite a rhetoric of subversion, it leads intellectuals down the path of acquiescence. Without an emphatic idea of freedom and happiness, a better society can scarcely be envisioned. (Jacoby, 1999, p. 136.)

As Shaughnessy and Sardoč's questions to Walzer as well as Walzer's replies illustrate, the political rhetoric that leads one towards a rejection of universals like truth, beauty, and justice *also* leads one towards the rejection of a vision of common citizenship that cuts across particularist identities and group interests. In both cases, the result is a misguided politics that slights what is common to us as human beings and what is common to us as citizens of a democratic polity. Radical multiculturalists need to reflect more deeply on the perils of jettisoning the very notion of a shared locus of civic agency.

## Notes

1. All page references in the text will be to this essay.
2. In this connection, it's clearly no accident that a leading civic republican like Michael Sandel goes out of his way to distance himself from a Rousseauian conception of general will; as Sandel understands quite well, an association with Rousseau's vision would quickly impugn civic republicanism as a contemporary political project. See Sandel, 1996, pp. 319–321, 347.
3. While Young allows that Barber frees himself from some of the worst deformities of Rousseau's exclusionary republicanism, she argues that Barber, no less than Rousseau, 'makes homogeneity a requirement of public participation' (p. 183).
4. Cf. p. 203, where Young speaks of an 'institutionalized right to veto policy proposals that directly affect [disadvantaged minorities]'. Brian Barry offers powerful arguments against Young's proposal in *Culture and Equality: An Egalitarian Critique of Multiculturalism* (Barry, 2001, pp. 302–305).
5. Just to elaborate a bit further on this example: according to Young's principles, religious extremists in Israel are to some extent an oppressed minority since they are culturally marginalized in relation to what is fundamentally a secular society. (Are *all* minorities in

some sense oppressed because their minority status in itself entails cultural marginalization?) But should that give these groups a license to flout principles of shared citizenship and block policies that would be good for the society as a whole? Giving them more 'voice' simply empowers them to disrupt the larger civic purposes of the society.

6. For a brief discussion of some problems in designing such a new regime, see Kymlicka, 1995, pp. 145–146.

7. For instance, she writes that there need to be fora for the self-organization of oppressed groups, where these groups would be 'able to discuss among themselves what procedures and policies they judge will best further their social and political equality', and mechanisms that would allow them 'to make their judgments known to the larger public' (p. 203). This suggests that the polity shared with other groups is *the place to which they bring their group demands*, rather than the place where citizens deliberate about what is best for all citizens.

8. It's important to qualify this by saying that Young never explicitly rules out the possibility of public-spirited dialogue between different groups (see p. 184). But the rhetoric of 'group-specific experience', and the presumption that appeals to a notion of common good are always a mere ruse that allows the dominant group to masquerade as the voice of a larger interest, tend to undercut public-spiritedness as a real possibility, even if she leaves open a bit of conceptual space for it to inhabit in principle. In any case, what will be the focus of this public-spiritedness if, as Young holds, the notion of a *civic* public is one that must be spurned?

9. To be sure, there is an element of this in all modern liberal politics. The question is whether various group identities merely qualify the core civic identity, or whether the civic identity defers entirely to more fundamental group identities.

10. For a particularly sophisticated set of debates, see Kelly, 2002.

11. On pp. 193–194, Young specifies those groups she sees as being 'clear candidates for group representation in policy making in the United States'. No one can deny that her list of 'clear candidates' (women, blacks, Native Americans, old people, poor people, disabled people, gay men and lesbians, Spanish-speaking Americans, young people, nonprofessional workers) is an expansive one.

12. See Kymlicka, 1995, p. 145; and Barry, 2002, p. 306 and p. 367, n. 50.

13. See Kymlicka & Norman, *Return of the Citizen*, p. 304. For a sharper statement of the same worry, see Barry, 2002, p. 21.

14. See Barry, 2002, pp. 11–12: 'The proliferation of special interests fostered by multicultural-ism is ... conducive to a politics of 'divide and rule' that can only benefit those who benefit most from the status quo. There is no better way of heading off the nightmare of unified political action by the economically disadvantaged that might issue in common demands than to set different groups of the disadvantaged against one another. Diverting attention away from shared disadvantages such as unemployment, poverty, low-quality housing and inadequate public services is an obvious long-term anti-egalitarian objective. Anything that emphasizes the particularity of each group's problems at the expense of a focus on the problems they share with others is thus to be welcomed. If political effort is dissipated in pressing for and defending special group privileges, it will not be available for mobilization on the basis of broader shared interests'. Jacoby, 1999, p. 58: 'What mangles people are bad or no jobs, decaying communities, tattered human relations and defective education rather than "misrecognition"'.

15. Cf. Jacoby, 1999 p. 11: 'The left once rejected pluralism as superficial; now it worships it as profound'. Young notes this shift in leftist politics on p. 185; in this sense, a theory like hers corresponds to Hegel's Owl of Minerva—that is, it seeks to articulate theoretically changes in thinking already embodied in actual social movements.

16. For a thorough analysis of these two cases, see Spinner, 1994, Chapter 5. As Spinner discusses, the dissimilarities between these two groups are instructive: although the Hasidim, like the Amish, are highly insular, unlike the Amish, they make eager use of their political rights. They do so, however, not in the spirit of democratic citizenship, but rather as a tool of group interests. Like the Israeli groups cited in note 5 above, the use (or abuse)

of bloc voting by the Hasidim presents itself as a kind of carrying-to-its-logical-limit (and hence parody) of group-based politics.

17. Having said that, I think one also needs to say that there is certainly something morally problematical in allowing these communities (for instance, the Amish) to reproduce their way of life by hampering the possibility of cultural exit on the part of their children through the expedient of limiting their education. On the other hand, if one responds to this moral problem by enforcing universal educational norms, then perhaps one isn't actually 'forcing them out of their culture', but one is certainly increasing their vulnerability to being swamped by the larger culture. I'm not sure there is any easy way around this dual quandary. Isn't the deliberate stunting of the educational horizons of their children too high a price to pay for the reproduction of a unique culture? This is without question a challenge that is not easily answered. It is on the basis of such considerations that Samuel Freeman writes: '*Yoder* is multiculturalism with a vengeance ... It preserves the Amish community at the expense of the civic freedom and individual development and independence of its members' (Freeman, 2002, p. 24).

18. See, for instance, Kymlicka and Norman, *Return of the Citizen*, p. 306. It is worth noting that Kymlicka and Norman, on the same page of their article, say that the fears on the part of critics of multiculturalism with respect to whether group rights undermine the integrative function of citizenship 'are *often* misplaced' (my italics); they do not make the ambitious claim that such fears are never warranted.

19. Cf. Kymlicka, 1995, p. 31: 'polyethnic rights are usually intended to promote integration into the larger society'.

20. Brian Barry nicely articulates the larger principle at stake here: 'I do not believe that governments can afford to accept fatalistically that some community can declare itself a burden on the rest of society in perpetuity on the basis of its culture. Moving towards an egalitarian liberal society is made enormously more problematic if it contains minority cultures whose members refuse to acknowledge that there are social obligations of citizenship as well as social rights' (Barry, 2002, p. 219).

21. See p. 190 ('most people tend to assert their own perspective as universal'), which is somewhat reminiscent of Hobbes's view of moral universals in *Leviathan*, Chapter 6. Cf Young, 1990, p. 97 ('the ideal of impartiality serves ideological functions. It masks the ways in which the particular perspectives of dominant groups claim universality'), pp. 115–116 (the 'propensity to universalize the particular'), as well as the epigraph from Michel Foucault on p. 96.

22. Young herself links together 'modern normative reason and its political expression in the idea of the civic public', and contends that the politics of difference must challenge or deconstruct both of them: see Young, 1990, p. 111.

23. In a recent interview, Young complains that the scope of what now gets discussed under the rubric of citizenship has expanded to the point where citizenship is no longer a particularly useful concept (Sardoč & Shaughnessy, 2001, p. 98), but it seems to me that there is nothing indeterminate in the meaning of the concept just specified.

24. Shaughnessy & Sardoč, 2001, p. 69. Walzer rightly considers himself to be a defender of multiculturalism, and yet throughout this interview he argues that the appropriate site for the reproduction of minority cultures is not the political realm (which is what the politics of recognition and the politics of difference would seem to require) but rather the 'private' sphere of 'families, churches, and ethnic associations' within the minority cultural community itself: see pp. 69–70.

## References

Barber, B. (1984) *Strong Democracy* (Berkeley, University of California Press).

Barry, B. (2001) *Culture and Equality: An Egalitarian Critique of Multiculturalism* (Cambridge, Polity Press).

Barry, B. (2002) Second Thoughts and Some First Thoughts Revived in: P. Kelly, (ed.), *Multiculturalism Reconsidered: Culture and Equality and its Critics* (Cambridge, Polity Press).

Freeman, S. (2002) Liberalism and the Accommodation of Group Claims in: P. Kelly, (ed.), *Multiculturalism Reconsidered: Culture and Equality and its Critics* (Cambridge, Polity Press).

Gitlin, T. (1996) *The Twilight of Common Dreams: Why America Is Wracked by Culture Wars* (Toronto, Owl Books).

Hobbes, T. *Leviathan*, ed. C. B. Macpherson (Harmondsworth, U.K., Penguin, 1968).

Jacoby, R. (1999) *The End of Utopia: Politics and Culture in an Age of Apathy* (New York, Basic Books).

Kelly, P. (ed.) (2002) *Multiculturalism Reconsidered: Culture and Equality and its Critics* (Cambridge, Polity Press).

Kymlicka, W. (1995) *Multicultural Citizenship: A Liberal Theory of Minority Rights* (Oxford, Clarendon Press).

Kymlicka, W. & Norman, W. (1995) Return of the Citizen: A Survey of Recent Work on Citizenship Theory in: R. Beiner, (ed.), *Theorizing Citizenship* (Albany, N.Y., State University of New York).

Rousseau, J-J. *On the Social Contract*, ed. Roger D. Masters, trans. Judith R. Masters (New York, St. Martin's Press, 1978).

Sandel, M. (1996) *Democracy's Discontent: America in Search of a Public Philosophy* (Cambridge, MA, Harvard University Press).

Sardoč, M. & Shaughnessy, M. F. (2001) An Interview with Iris Marion Young, *Educational Philosophy and Theory*, 33:1.

Shaughnessy, M. F. & Sardoč, M. (2002) An Interview with Michael Walzer, *Studies in Philosophy and Education*, 21:1.

Spinner, J. (1994) *The Boundaries of Citizenship: Race, Ethnicity, and Nationality in the Liberal State* (Baltimore, The Johns Hopkins University Press).

Young, I. M. (1990) *Justice and the Politics of Difference* (Princeton, N.J., Princeton University Press).

Young, I. M. (1995) Polity and Group Difference: A Critique of the Ideal of Universal Citizenship, in: R. Beiner, (ed.), *Theorizing Citizenship* (Albany, N.Y., State University of New York).

# 3
# Iris Marion Young and Political Education

ELIZABETH FRAZER
*University of Oxford*

## Introduction

This paper falls into two main parts. First I set out an interpretive analysis of Iris Young's theory of politics. Second I consider what this theory of politics suggests relative to political education.

My account of Young's theory of politics is interpretive because Young, like many current political theorists, does not bring politics as such as a process or a practice into clear and sustained analytic focus; although of course her work on justice, equality, communication, public life and so on is profoundly significant for our understanding of what politics is and what it ought to be. Iris Young's work is avowedly methodologically and theoretically eclectic. In the spirit of *critical theory* she is always concerned to expose what material interests are served by theories and philosophies. So for example, her discussion of humanist and gynocentric feminisms focuses on the material implications of these two approaches (Young, 1990b, pp. 4, 73–91). She discusses the 'ideological effects' of the interest group pluralism theory that frames much political science and political theory (1990a, pp. 74–75); and she interrogates the ideological effects of the ideal of impartiality (1990a, pp. 111–116). Crucially, for her, critical theory is transformative and engaged—it offers alternative visions of social relations (1990a, p. 226). It is avowedly socially situated (2000, p. 10) and hence cannot pretend to abstract objectivity or detachment. She also frequently deploys a *phenomenological method* which aims, among other things, to uncover the texture of the lived life. Young uses this method to explore what it is like to be relatively powerless or powerful in a social setting, as in her discussion of 'throwing like a girl' (1990b, pp. 141–159) and later in her normative theory of recognition and greeting (1997, p. 57) and her analysis of the group connected experience of being regarded by others with aversion (1990a, p. 123). She also uses some of the apparatus of the *deconstructive approach* which emphasizes the impossibility of a closed or wholly stable analysis of concepts (2000, p. 127). The philosophical method of deconstruction has its counterpart in social theory, where we should expect incompleteness, openness, and discontinuities.

Her methodological and theoretical presuppositions are hostile to systematic theory in its traditional sense of a structured set of concepts and hypothesized causal connections and logical implications, which aspires to completeness and positive testability (1990b, p. 52). Indeed, Young is constantly pointing to the constructive and indeed oppressive uses to which theory, thought of that way, is put. For example, the theories of 'interest group pluralism' which dominate political science and theory paint a picture of a 'depoliticized public life'. To the extent that theory guides action the model has an actually depoliticizing effect (1990a, p. 72). Similarly, in normative political theory the focus on the just distribution of material and other goods turns both theoretical and practical attention from the contexts and causes of the power mechanisms and inequalities that channel flows of goods (1990a, p. 134).

Clearly, it misrepresents Young to lay out a set of concepts, logical connections and hypothetical causal relations. Such 'formalism' runs counter to her methodological commitments. Nevertheless we can validly consider her central concepts and interpret her understanding of the nature of politics as a practice. In the second part I consider recent debates about 'teaching citizenship' and consider how such a project might change in order to meet the conditions of Young's models of heterogeneous publics and pluralistic politics.

To anticipate my detailed discussion, I believe there are two related tensions in Young's theory of politics, and that these reflect a tension in politics itself. The first tension is that:

- On the one hand, individuals' and groups' legitimate claims to recognition and political rights, and their justification of political action, proceed from their social needs.
- On the other hand, Young's theory of politics emphasizes the importance of coalitions and allegiances across differences.
- The legitimacy of coalition claims and actions, however, cannot proceed directly from the needs of their members, as can (according to Young) the legitimacy of group claims. So we need an independent justification for coalition action.

There is a gap, then, in her theory of political legitimacy. The second tension is that:

- Young emphasizes strategic competition between groups. Her theory is that groups have political capacity, the capacity to produce political power. Individuals and groups are not wholly constrained by their structural position.
- On the other hand, her political theory emphasizes the obligation that groups have to transfer resources and rights to more disadvantaged groups, the obligation of the powerful to listen, to communicate with, and to respect, the disadvantaged, the marginal and the oppressed.
- The problem is that the theory of politics leaves it unclear why, in any actual political situation, these obligations of justice should prevail over the logic of political struggle. If groups are to struggle for recognition, rights and advantage, the logic is that other groups—including the more powerful—should struggle back.

There is a problem, then, in Young's theory of the relationship between ethics and politics.

Arguably, both these gaps and problems should be resolvable by way of the theory of justice. Justice is the phenomenon that yokes together politics and ethics and holds them in balance or harmony. But in Iris Young's theory of justice questions about what justice requires are addressed by way of the theory of groups. So displacing the problem from the relationship between ethics and politics (where I have located it in this essay) to the theory of justice would only reiterate the problem, not resolve it.

I believe that these tensions in theoretical understanding of the relation between ethics and politics mirror real tension in institutions and practices of politics. This is a tension that political education projects cannot evade.

## 1. Young's Theory of Politics

Iris Young can be read as engaged, in part, in a project of *reclaiming politics* both as an academic study and a practical endeavour. She seeks to reclaim it from academic and practical emphases on the established framework of institutions, constitutions and laws. This does not mean that institutions, constitutions and laws are of no interest. On the contrary, Young more than many other contemporary political theorists, brings the aspirational and envisioning aspects of critical theory together with a concrete attention to existing institutional contexts and to possible transformations of these. She also emphasizes the need to shift from an ethical analysis of just distributions to a political analysis of 'procedural issues of participation in deliberation and decision making' (1990a, p. 34). Young's work, like many feminists', sees no alternative to a thoroughgoing combination of moral, social and political theory. Her central focus is on *values* as these interact with concrete *social and political relationships*, and on the possible *political transformation* of this complex structure.

Like a number of other political theorists writing in the last decades of the twentieth century Young is concerned with the *depoliticization* of contemporary life. She calls, for example, for a *repoliticized public sphere*. What does she mean by this? For Iris Young, on my interpretation, the field and practice of politics is the field and practice of the *use and deployment of cooperative power by individuals in groups to intervene in the patterns of power in their society.* This is my formulation, not hers, and it is the synoptic result of reading her work with particular attention to the theory of politics (rather than, say, her philosophical anthropology, or epistemology, or ethics). I shall discuss each element of this formulation before returning to the question of what repoliticization would be.

The first, and central, element is *individuals in groups*. Society, for Young, is made up of individuals, groups, series, associations and aggregations. Not all political actors are groups. For example, 'women' are best conceptualized as a *series* in Sartre's sense (1997, pp. 12–37). Series can be individuated (for example, the queue outside the club, women, the working class). Individuals are positioned within a series by virtue of norms and expectations, and the interaction between individual lives and social structures. (For example, your behaviour is conditioned by your being third in the bus queue. Your being third in the bus queue is the upshot of contingency and the interaction of many individual decisions.) When so positioned our relationship to fellow series members is distinctly different from our relationship to individuals who are not members of the series. The members of a series can act collectively. (For example, the people in the bus queue can cooperate to call and share a taxi if the bus doesn't come.) Often, though, individual members of series act independently, and the upshot can frequently be unintended and damaging. (For example, when everyone steps forward at once so nobody can get on to the bus until the series cooperates to regroup) (1997, p. 25). None of this in the least implies that our identities are determined, or exhausted, or even constructed, by the series or our membership of it (2000, pp. 100–101). Similarly, *associations* are important political actors. In associations individuals get together voluntarily in order to pursue shared projects and interests (2000, pp. 160–164). Associations will be important actors in any repoliticized public life (2000, pp. 173–180). However, associations can construct themselves as *interest groups* in order to compete politically in a context in which those who lack the necessary organisational resources will be doubly disadvantaged. This is one of the fatal flaws in 'interest group pluralism' in which self-constituted interest groups win power and influence consonant with their organisational and other material resources—it precisely leaves the distribution of resources as it is.

*Groups* are the effect of power in a different way from associations and series. Powerful groups are advantaged by the structures of power; powerless groups are disadvantaged, oppressed, excluded and exploited by it (1990a, pp. 48–63). From the point of view of members—one 'finds oneself' as a member of group, in contrast to both associations and series (1990a, p. 46) and group membership is overwhelmingly fateful for individuals. One can hardly be unconscious of one's group membership as one can of one's membership of a series; but one is not conscious of it in the same way as one is conscious of one's membership of an association one has voluntarily joined. In one place Young says that she reserves the term group for the 'self-consciously mutually acknowledging collective with a self-conscious purpose' (1997, p. 23). In another she says that 'oppression happens to social groups' (1990a, p. 9). This means, it happens to groups and members of groups, not to individuals as such. That is, one individual can be pushed around by another individual or group; to be oppressed is to be oppressed not as an individual as such but as a member of a group. And by extension we can infer that exploitation, oppression, marginalisation and exclusion are done by groups, not by individuals.

Young's theory of groups is relational. This theory of difference does not imply that:

> groups lie outside one another. To say that there are differences among groups does not imply that there are not overlapping experiences, or that two groups have nothing in common. The assumption that real differences in affinity, culture, or privilege imply oppositional categorisation must be challenged (1990a, p. 171).

There is, similarly, no implication that individuals' identities are wholly or even overwhelmingly constructed by their group membership—individuals have multiple positions in group differentiated relations (2000, pp. 100; 139). This is quite consistent, of course, with individuals' being treated, and treating each other, according to perceived group membership. It is this aspect of group life that means that the relative advantage or disadvantage of groups is of first political and ethical importance. Members of advantaged groups can voluntarily associate to further their interests; they can consciously construct themselves as interest groups in order to compete politically (2000, p. 90). Disadvantaged, exploited and oppressed groups are likely to be deprived of the material resources that are necessary for this voluntary association and organisation.

When acting politically, groups, associations and series use and deploy *cooperative power*. Young's illustrative examples of democratic politics in action emphasize the capacities that people have when they organize, coordinate, and act together (2000, pp. 1–3; 1997, pp. 12–13, 161; 1990a, pp. 83–88). And this cooperative power is deployed to intervene in patterns of power—the power to decide, to distribute, to dominate, to govern. Again, I extract this formulation not from any formal analysis of political action, but from Young's illustrative examples of political action in the context of welfare states (1990b, p. 55; 1990a, pp. 81–88), the relationship between socialist and anti-capitalist politics and the commitment to women's liberation (1990b, p. 30), and the relationship between politics in civil society and anti-bureaucratic and anti-capitalist action (1990b, p. 92; 2000, pp. 174–180). In all these cases, Young's analysis has a twin emphasis. First, on the structure of power and the normative justification of this structure in dominant discourses and theories. Second, on the phenomenology of resistance and solidarity on the part of people engaged and enmeshed in these structures.

The final element of my formulation of Young's concept of politics is that individuals in groups intervene in patterns of power *in their society*. It is important to emphasize that for Young the important power, the power that is valuable and which is causally important, is social. Certainly the relationships and differences Young analyses are social—which category encompasses sex, gender, sexuality, religion, ethnicity, and culture (2000, p. 81). For her, the interesting aspect of politics is its interaction with society—the interesting political claims are those that are asserted from or mesh with social positions (2000, p. 82). Young presumes, I think, that social relations, social groups and social differences could exist without a *polity*, and without *political institutions*—while the converse is conceptually incoherent. She presumes, I think, although this is nowhere explicit, that wherever there are social relations there will be conflict and individuals will find collective power to bring to bear on the structures of domination that govern them. We can call this process politics. She strongly resists the idea that in order to bring political power properly to bear on social relations, distributions, conflicts and so on we must construct institutions of political power and procedures of political decision making that are in any sense autonomous of society, or that we must in political decision making abstract away from social positions, or that in entering the forum we should leave our social identities (together with our swords and guns) outside. That is, Young has a concept and a theory of politics that is thoroughgoingly *social*:

> Politics. ... concerns all aspects of institutional organisation, public action, social practices and habits, and cultural meanings insofar as they are potentially subject to collective evaluation and decision making (1990a, pp. 9, 34).

We must now turn to other salient elements of what we can think of as Young's theory of politics. On my reading these are polity, publicity, representation, authorisation, accountability and equality and justice. I shall set these out in turn.

A *polity* is a collective whose members recognize themselves to be governed by common rule-making and negotiating procedures (2000, p. 27). These common institutions of governance—such things as parliaments, magistracies, prefectures—are sufficient for polity. Young is concerned to deny that a polity either is or should be anything like the 'political community' that is so common in recent political theory. A polity is not nor should it be tied by shared norms, values, ways of life, ethnicities, national identities, language, culture, religion or history (1997, p. 67; 2000, p. 29). The *point* of a polity is that it can hold together a population who do not share any of these. But a flourishing and just democratic polity must be held together by *publicity*. In a democratic and just polity the governing institutions are public. To count as public (adjective) an event or institution must be open to everyone (no one can be excluded), it must be accessible to everyone (conditions must be such that it is actually possible for all to enter), it must be publicly visible and audible—that is to say, reported, broadcast and otherwise covered by public media such as the press, the internet and so on (1990b, p. 107). The, or a, public (noun) is the members of the polity visible and audible to each other. Contrary to a good deal of recent political theory there is no requirement that a public be uniform, homogeneous, or in agreement about anything apart from the fact that particular institutions govern them (although there need be no agreement that these institutions are as they should be) (1990b, p. 8; 1990a, p. 7; 2000, pp. 111–112). Public life is one bit of life where we encounter people who are different or strange; where we are challenged; where we are not understood. Public life is messy (2000, p. 168). It is risky and to this degree erotic (1990a, pp. 240–241).

The next salient elements of Young's theory of politics are *representation and authorisation*. Representation, again contrary to a good deal of recent political theory, does not require shared identity. And representation must be tied to authorisation. Although clearly there is a sense in which a representative's claim to act on behalf of some group is partially constitutive of that group it cannot be fully constitutive absent members' own reflexive constitution of themselves as that group and their authorisation of the representation. Authorisation and group constitution are intimately linked (2000, pp. 3–4, 21–130ff). Representation, then, is a differentiation among political actors (2000, p. 127).

Young does not say in so many words, as do some political theorists, that the end of politics is justice. To say such a thing would be altogether too essentialist and abstract about concepts. In any case, her method seems to be based on the principle that ethics is analytically distinct from both politics and the social while at the same time the three must be kept together by theorists (2000, p. 11). On this reading, the values of equality and publicity can be understood to frame—and constrain—political action and political institutions. But the closeness of the relation between *politics and justice* looks rather more radical if we attend to such remarks as 'the concept of justice is coextensive with the political' (1990a, p. 9) and that there is a 'correspondence between polity and justice' (2000, p. 27). Justice is not only the proper egalitarian distribution of burdens and benefits among groups and individuals, but is distinctly concerned with the full recognition of each group and individual as a worthy and rightful member of the society and polity, and with the lifting of any structures of domination, exploitation or exclusion.

If justice is to be realized there are a number of concrete constraints on individual and group action *vis-à-vis* others. First, careful attention must be paid to the norms of public communication—particularly respect for the being, and the voices, of others (2000, pp. 55ff, 168). This respect and recognition is not based on what we might call homophily—or recognition of and therefore favour for those who are like us. Instead, it must be based on our capacity to recognize what is different about others, our capacity to recognize what value commitments, ways of life, histories and cultures, divide us from each other, yet across which differences communication is, with care and trouble, still possible.

Second, justice requires norms, institutions, procedures, and above all, public spaces for *accountability*. Accountability is our political way of securing justice (2000, pp. 173–180). Again, at the risk of presenting Young's theory more formally than she intends, we can interpret from her work a model of lines of accountability that run in different directions: lines from representative to represented and back again (2000, pp. 128–133), between citizens in groups and decision makers so that decision makers have to account to groups how proposed policies would affect those groups (1990b, p. 124; 1990a, pp. 184–186), and between groups of citizens (1997, p. 68). Traditional political science and political theory fail really to get to grips with accountability, according to Young. The tradition of communicative ethics which is often employed by discursive democrats to ground their procedural theory, is overly fixated on rational and formal modes of discourse to the exclusion of the uses of language, such as narrative and diverse rhetorical forms, that are also political resources (1997, pp. 69–74; 2000, pp. 57–77). Exclusive modes of language are one of the most potently coercive weapons in the hands (or mouths) of the powerful. Requirements that individuals use only set modes of address, a fixed vocabulary, or an esoteric code are all discursive devices commonly used in legislatures, courtrooms, committees, councils, professional groups, corporations, and, of course, in subcultures and dominant cultures. They are very efficient ways of maintaining hierarchies, marking and socialising members, and intimidating newcomers and outsiders. Young argues that in a truly democratic polity it is incumbent on the relatively powerful to listen to the voices of the less powerful which means hearing diverse and unfamiliar voices speaking in strange ways (2000, pp. 80, 112; 1997, pp. 6–7). Communicative ethics should not enjoin us to 'take up the standpoint of the other'. Such a prescription presupposes an overly simple and straightforward human capacity to swap social positions. Instead Young sketches a theory of what she calls 'asymmetrical reciprocity', which emphasizes the partial and incomplete nature of exchange, the always elusive nature of understanding, the fragility and provisionality of communication. But we do have the capacity to acknowledge and take account of the other (1997, p. 41). All of this adds up to a model of public, political life, which cannot be a 'comfortable place of conversation among those who share language, assumptions and ways of looking at issues' (2000, p. 111). Accountability, based as it is in communication, must be a frictional, conflictual, and partial process.

An important and controversial element of Young's theory of politics is her proposed principle of group representation, according to which a democratic public should provide mechanisms for the effective representation and recognition of distinct voices and perspectives of those of its constituent groups that are oppressed and disadvantaged within it (1990a, pp. 184–191; 2000, pp. 141–148). She proposes that disadvantaged groups should have the power of veto over proposals that affect them adversely, as well as public resources for self-organisation (1990b, p. 124).

There are a number of points to make about this. First, it enjoins on policy making a highly sophisticated level and application of understanding of social structures and social relations, networks and groups. Second, it requires a flexible set of institutions and procedures of accountability—flexible enough to keep up with changing social relations and structures. Third, it raises the question of the tension, already mentioned, between two aspects of Young's theory of politics. These are, first, that aspect of her theory of groups which emphasizes that members of a group share needs and interests, stemming from some aspect of their structural position, especially the way they are treated in the society and polity. It is from this fateful aspect of group membership that the principle of group representation is justified. Second, though, Young's theory of politics is a theory of strategic action, and especially, of coalitions and alliances between multiply positioned individuals (2000, pp. 139–141; 1990b, pp. 9–10). Patterns of political actions do not follow straightforwardly from social positions. Instead politics is the outcome of strategic considerations about bases for mobilisation, relations with other social and political campaigns and movements. This is clearly true of women's politics (1990b, p. 30). But it also follows from her relational theory of groups in general. Private mumblings and a sense of discontent and disadvantage can generate organisation among social actors and the formation of an oppositional political formation whose precise shape depends on the contingencies of the political context. Indeed, the shape of such a political formation can take the form of what Young calls 'subaltern counterpublics' (2000, p. 172).

The tension here can be seen as one between two theories of political legitimacy—between legitimacy stemming from social need, and legitimacy stemming from political practice, in particular, strategic action. The first theory is that political mobilisation and action can be generated out of shared needs and interests. These shared needs and interests, and in particular the group's position in a structure of disadvantage, are the reasons which justify and ground claims for particular consideration. To meet the conditions of democratic justice these claims must be made publicly, in a political setting in which a group's members or their representatives set out the salient reasons for a particular decision. In the democratic polity the group and representatives know they will be heard as full members of the society and the polity, and accorded the respect that status involves. It is possible to read Young's principle of group representation as implying that the group's shared disadvantage, its voice, and its authorisation of its representatives, are themselves counters in the justification of the group's demands. Another way of putting the point is that the group's social ontology is the key counter in the justification of its political action and claims.

The second theory of legitimacy is that political power is generated out of strategic action and especially coalition and alliance building. Young's social theory emphasizes that individuals have complex group memberships and allegiances. This means that there must be an element of strategy both in the political construction of a group—that is, in the decision of group members to authorize representatives and to act politically—and in the cooperation between groups in the formation of a political coalition or alliance. Political action does not, then, follow straightforwardly from social position. Instead, strategic considerations govern decisions about alliances such as that between feminism and the gay movement, or between migrants and people of colour in some setting of ethnic competition. In this kind of case the legitimacy of a coalition's claims does not stem from the coalition members' shared disadvantage and needs. Such shared disadvantage and needs might be one counter in an argument, but a coalition's opponents are surely justified in attempting to drive a wedge between coalition members—precisely to disaggregate the needs claims.

Another way of expressing this problem is as follows. If groups are 'given', and individuals 'find themselves' in them, then according to Young this fact about individual and group identity justifies special political measures for compensation, rights and so on. But if, to the contrary, groups are strategic, and based on the exploitation of political potential and power by their members collectively, it is not clear why any other group in the polity should concede any special political recognition, compensation or rights. If power underpins group action, then why should we not leave the outcome to the political process itself? If groups are politically constructed, the dealings between them, it might be argued, are political dealings.

A conventional answer to this question is that politics must be constrained by justice. But Young's theory of justice itself contains the very problem I have identified. Justice is distinctly concerned with the full recognition of each group and individual as a worthy and rightful member of the society and polity. But this means that the theory of groups is an essential constituent of the theory of justice. We shall return in what follows to the question of the relative roles of political power and ethics in Young's theory.

## 2. Political Education

In this section I discuss, first, some general problems with 'political education' and 'education for citizenship'—some of the problems that make these topics for continued debate among both political theorists and educators. Second, I turn to the question of what content and form political education should have were we to aspire to Young's model of political life. Third, I link this programme for education back to some specific problems about the delivery of political education, and then to questions about the relationship between society, polity, and ethics.

## Problems of Political Education

There are several reasons why political education and 'citizenship education' pose distinct difficulties beyond the general pedagogical problems of how children, young people and adults learn, and the relationships between formal instruction, skills acquisition, and knowledge and understanding. Elsewhere I have argued that a particular problem for education for citizenship, or political education, is that in many polities citizens including teachers are very unclear about *what politics, as such, means* (Frazer, 2000). In particular, it is a rare group of citizens which has had the opportunity to think systematically about what a world or a society without politics would be like and what, by contrast, the particular values of politics are. In discussions of politics negative values—associations between politics and petty partisanship, dissimulation, endless argument for argument's sake, and the love of power for its own sake—are often uppermost and citizens find it difficult to articulate any positive values of political process as a counterweight to these negatives. Discussion of such values as publicity, open conflict, deliberation, civility, inclusion and so on, predictably enough, invite sceptical if not downright cynical responses about politics as it actually is as opposed to politics as it ought to be. Even more notable, it is not clear to many citizens—and we should remember, neither is it clear to many political theorists—that there is any clear content to the idea of *politics as it should be*. For many political theorists and philosophers, politics is as it is. The important thing is that it should be constrained by morality. By logic, though, if we can talk of the corruption of politics we must be committed to some normative model of *politics uncorrupted* (Philp, 1997, pp. 446–448). Some political theorists— Young among them—analyse politics in such a way as to illuminate values that are inherent in the political process itself. But the question of what values are intrinsic to or immanent in politics, is undoubtedly more uncertain, more contested, and subject to more scepticism, even than questions about values in other domains of life.

Next, more than most subjects, education for citizenship and political education are *politically controversial*. According to some critics this is because it is a 'nonsubject'—the kind of general life skill that has no place on the formal curriculum, although of course life in school or in any other educational institution gives occasions for learning, and political education can be identified as a feature of the hidden or informal curriculum (Pring, 1999). It can also be because it is thought to be a biased subject, a subject that is an occasion for ideology or brainwashing, one that gives educators too much social power, especially over young people. It is true that in many societies 'politics' smacks overwhelmingly of partisanship. If politics is equated with partisanship then proscriptions on partisanship will be proscriptions on politics as such.

One possible inference from these considerations is that political education should not be undertaken in schools and colleges, but should be left to other social institutions. Parties, pressure groups, social movements, interest groups and other explicitly political organisations should be the site of this education. In these settings partisan identity has already been consciously elected by members, which removes any worry about 'bias' or 'ideology'. From deliberately elected partisan standpoints members can learn about institutions, values, procedures and skills. However, if political education is engaged in only by political organisations, then only a very small proportion of citizens will receive any political education at all. Further, such education is unlikely to be systematic, as it is not political organisations' main task. Finally, it might be thought education from such a particular point of view does not meet the need for education of citizens from the point of view of democratic politics as such.

From the point of view of democracy itself there are several educational requirements. First, there is a requirement for the *socialisation of full political members*— citizens with all the capacities for judgement, action, and government that that status entails. This requirement does not necessarily involve any formal curriculum slot. Participation, cooperation, a habit of enquiry, critical capacity, a sense of justice: all are skills and intellectual capacities gainable by participation in a school, college, or university, or indeed in other social organisations like firms, if they are themselves organized along democratic and participatory lines, and if members have responsibilities of judgement and decision making.

Second, though, citizens must understand the *structure, constitution and institutions* that govern them. The institutional framework, the conduct of the partisan competition for the power to govern, the constitution and its transformations, the interrelationships between these things and a country's or region's history and society is a perfectly good academic subject. However, in those school systems (such as the US) where most schools make a serious effort to teach the subject, it is often criticized for being dull and boring, and as subjects go it has a reputation for being rather ineffective. Third, some democratic theorists argue that it is less the institutions and more the concomitant *values* that are important. This raises the question whether 'teaching values' has any place in the formal curriculum or whether it is rather a matter of the whole school ethos, and a feature of the informal curriculum. Fourth, there is a need for citizens to get to grips with the *ideas of politics and democratic government* and the values and prescriptions for human and social relationships inherent in those practices and institutions. I would add that citizens have also to understand and be able to evaluate the constraints on their lives in a polity—some of which are grounded in a logic of the power to govern. The dynamics of this power are inevitably less transparent and more perverse than is idealized in democratic theory. The point here is that political education cannot be thought of as 'socialisation' into lived values and practices. Deliberate articulation and critical understanding of the workings of political power are a necessary element of the living of its values.

Fifth, taking up the 'political point of view' also involves *telling a power story*—a story or stories of the polity, and the settlement such as it is. Iris Young is only one of many political and social theorists who expresses severe misgivings about this enterprise (1990a, p. 157). Any such story that is constructed will immediately trigger energetic criticism and dissent. Athough educators should not shrink, presumably, from the task of guiding students through controversy and conflict, the presentation of a story of a society that is cut with conflict and division, exploitation and oppression, disadvantage and exclusion, is a difficult project. The alternative—and this is more or less the tack that has been taken in numerous current citizenship education programmes (Torney-Purta *et al.*, 1999)—is to tell a story of a basically unified polity in which a more nearly just society has been established over time, emphasising the structure of opportunity for citizens' participation in their society. The turn to 'citizenship education' from 'political education' is focused, in part, on increasing citizens' and young people's sense of political efficacy, their sense that it is worth acting in support of causes and values that they cherish, and in pursuit of justice. The difficulty with this is that the unavoidable element of dissimulation, the superficiality of apparent order and agreement, that is arguably at the heart of all politics, invites scepticism towards politics and citizenship themselves.

Perhaps more than with other subjects, therefore, politics requires educators and learners to address uncertainty, contestation and non-completion. I shall return to the question of how this can be done in the final section of this essay. First, we turn to the question what Iris Young's particular theory of politics requires of political education.

### Education for Young's Polity

Iris Young's political theory, in my interpretation, points educators to the instilling and development of a particular set of skills in political actors. If citizens and young citizens are to learn how to use and deploy cooperative power in order to intervene in the structures of power in society, then some peculiar topics and principles have to be addressed. First, the social bases for political action, as we have seen, according to Young, consist of *social groups* and *coalitions and alliances* of individuals and groups. The polity consists of just those groups and individuals who share governing institutions, and the workings of these institutions must be constrained by the principles of *publicity* and of *justice*—it is not the case, in her polity, that anything goes. The basis of these values and principles, in turn, is not rooted in any deeply shared culture or way of life. They are based, rather, in the political fact of *shared decision making and governing institutions.*

Earlier I identified a problem in the detail of Young's theory of the relationship between justice and politics. In my view, resolution of this problem, theoretically, will bring the phenomenology and concept of politics more sharply into focus, in its own terms, than Young and other contemporary political theorists are wont to do. I must take a shortcut here as there is inadequate space to fully work out the implications of what I have just said. But if I am right, one implication is that citizens and educators must be ready to address the question of *education for politics*, not just education for *citizenship* or even education for *democracy.*

So, what political skills must, by implication from Young's theory, be acquired in education? First, the *articulation of one's own cultural, social, moral, political, ethnic, religious, and personal values and* identity in a way that is as authentic as possible.

Second, citizens have to learn to *communicate the truth of these values* and identity to others who, in the first place, do not share them, and further might be anti-pathetic to them. Young is clearly not in favour of teaching all citizens a common mode of discourse and address. This would run counter to her theory of a hetero-geneous polity, a polity furthermore that is open and accessible to newcomers, unassimilated groups and those who have not had the benefit of full education within the social and political system Nevertheless, the unassimilated must be educated into the polity to the extent that members are able to authorize repre-sentatives to speak for them and pursue their interests, and to the extent that these representatives can speak publicly in order to address the polity. Third, there is the reciprocal obligation to *learn how to listen* to, and to hear, the voices, stories, narratives, protests, and indeed values and identities of others, delivered in diverse voices, voices that are unfamiliar. Citizens have to learn to attempt to understand what these voices are saying and where they are coming from. That is, in Young's political theory a key political skill is communication across heterogeneity and openness to unassimilated others.

Fourth, citizens have to learn that *oppression is to be resisted politically*. People in groups who recognize themselves to be disadvantaged have to know how to resist. Education must have a part to play in the development of consciousness about oppression. Citizens have to develop the capacity for voice and communication. A number of anecdotal discussions in Young's essays indicate the importance of writing, speaking, meeting, leafleting, campaigning, petitioning, demonstrating, and so on.

One of the key aspects of politics that arises out of this and the foregoing analysis of Young's work is that politics is fraught with tensions. These tensions pose diffi-culties for political education that compound those already identified in the previous section. We now meet again the tensions between on the one hand *the logic of political strategy*, and on the other hand the *ethical significance of fateful social identities*, and the tension between those two and the commitment to *shared institutions and public communication*. In my view, whatever the upshot of attempts to resolve these tensions philosophically and theoretically, they must be lived and worked out practically. The implications of that, though, for 'teaching politics' needs careful thought.

As we saw, Young's theory implies that one justification of special claims by and rights for disadvantaged groups is that the group members share a place in the structure of disadvantage. On the other hand, Young is at pains to ensure that we do not read this as a theory of clearly bounded groups, monologically constructed individual social identities, or fixed political affiliations. The logic both of political strategy and of public heterogeneity is that political power is effectively deployed in coalitions, alliances, and shifting movements. However, there is no doubt that the workings of political strategy, the making and unmaking of alliances, destabilizes any straightforward translation of social structural position to the justified political construction of a public claim. The claim of a disadvantaged group, for example a recently migrant ethnic group who share the fate of some particular housing and labour market segment, is justified politically by, and is debatable at the bar of public communication by reference to, just that disadvantaged position. But the coalition of that group with some other, say a party, or a pressure group, or even another disadvantaged group, significantly alters the social ontology that justified the claim and guarantees the hearing in the first place. Yoking political positions together cannot help but affect the reception of claims by the coalition's fellow (but rival) citizens. This, of course, is why coalition and alliance is the very stuff of politics, and the interaction between force, effectiveness, and moral standing is what fascinates spectators and participants alike in political competition.

There is a parallel tension between political strategy and the democratic commitment to shared governing institutions and publicity constrained by justice. As we have seen Young definitely resists the classical political solution of 'citizen virtue' or a seamless public culture which instantiates and institutionalizes the virtues of the polity. Even so, there is a serious question, not easy on my reading of Young's work to answer, about the extent to which she is satisfied if the commitment to the governing institutions and procedures is itself only strategic. That Young might be constrained to be satisfied with this is suggested by her theory of quite radical heterogeneity, and asymmetric and partial understanding between citizens. All this suggests that we are in no position to pronounce normatively on what, phenomenologically let alone formally, counts as ethical commitment. So, by extension we are in no position to cast critical judgement on the nature, the depth, the authenticity or what have you of any other group's or individual's ethical commitment to the polity (providing, that is, that they are playing the game acceptably at the level of performance). On the other hand, that a group's or section's commitment to polity should be contingent on their continued political success or dominance—fine though that may be for a certain kind of political 'realist'—does not seem to meet Young's ethical argument about the values of publicity and justice.

How should a teacher tackling 'citizenship education' in the classroom, or an educator addressing 'politics' approach these tensions? And how can these vital political skills—voice, listening, strategy and all the rest—be learned? Here is not the place to engage in course or curriculum design. But in my view Iris Young's work, like other seriously *political* political theories, gives us some vital ideas as to why political education is difficult and how these difficulties can be tackled. To begin with, it seems to me, that any presentation of a polity as a smoothly running system for the decontestation of options and the peaceful resolution of conflict simply invites a cynical response whether from the young or from adult citizens. At the centre of politics is the partial resolution of conflict, the deferral of problems, misunderstanding (whether the result of serious attempts to understand or not), the public encounter between antagonists, and the continual challenge to governors who might, or might not, genuinely be doing their best but who can expect no thanks either way. Clearly some teachers who dedicate their efforts to sustained attempts to build confidence, to instil a sense of efficacy and the capacity to win victories in cooperation with others, will find the prospect of tackling this essentially tragic flaw at the centre of our society very daunting.

The answer, it seems to me, is two-fold. First, is to ask 'if not this, then what?'. There are, extant, a whole range of alternatives to political government. For instance, in many versions the ideal of community in which we all agree on basic ways of life and values, in which individuals are socialized to put the good of the community before their own good, is a project of eliminating or overcoming the inconsistency, coercion, conflict, irresolution and general messiness of politics. Arguments for strong authoritarian leadership, similarly. So too is the ideal of a society based on free exchanges between individuals—the libertarian or market utopia in which the coercion of political authority and the corruption of government has been evaded. Serious thought about these alternatives—their values, their advantages and disadvantages, their consequences for individuals and groups—has the advantage, in my experience, of focusing minds on the values of politics.

Second, the skills of listening to voices one finds difficult to understand, of trying to resolve conflicts not to everyone's satisfaction but with a partial solution that all can continue to live with until there is an occasion to revisit the decision or re-open the conflict, of articulating one's own convictions and needs in such a way that they can be heard in a public setting: all of these are skills that can be practiced in classrooms and workshops and other training and educational settings.

*Political education, society and ethics*

All of the foregoing, I hope, is making it clear how we need a specifically political education. Politics and citizenship cannot simply emerge from an education in social values and ethics. The political way of organising society is not simply inferrable from any understanding of social structure and social and economic relationships. Clearly, an ethical education that encompasses theories of justice is a necessary condition for citizenship in a just society. But it is hardly sufficient. The necessary supplement is an explicitly political education which enables citizens to think about the political pursuit of justice. That is, politics is quite distinct from ethics. Far from the two collapsing, or our not being able to treat one without the other, we have to keep them apart.

The same is true for the distinction between political and social theory. Although Young, like many recent political theorists, insists that these two are and must be yoked together, nevertheless, they are not just reflexes of one another. Think back to the theory of social ontology and the construction of a political group. Young's argument is that a group is a plurality of individuals who share a common position in the structure of advantage and share consciousness of the ties between. In certain circumstances this social ontology can be constructed, by way of authorisation and the articulation of aspirations politically, into a political group. What constraints are there on the conduct of the group in the process of this political construction and thereafter? In Young's theory there are ethical constraints—precisely the constraints of justice. But for her, justice is a political construction in the sense that it is to be pursued politically, and it is to be realized by way of political values such as transparency and publicity, equal participation and respect in public, and the public articulation of a commitment to the removal of disadvantage, exploitation, oppression and marginalisation.

The interesting problem that Young's political theory poses—and it is one that we must take most seriously—is how to secure a polity within which the advantaged recognize their special responsibility to ensure the recognition, voice, and indeed veto power, of the disadvantaged, without lapsing into the kind of practices of 'noblesse oblige' or discourses of unity that has been the most common solution to this problem but which, in Young's view, simply compound an injustice with a falsehood. That is, the polity is rooted in society—and society as it is, not as it might be. The polity consists of those who share governing institutions—there is no pretence that they share ways of life, or languages, or even values, beyond those that are directly implied by the shared institutions. Rather, those who share governing institutions, notwithstanding the political values of publicity and justice and the workings of political institutions that instantiate and model these values, actually have antagonistic interests, identities, discourses, conceptions of the good life etc.

Another aspect of Young's theory that turns us to the specificity of politics is that we should not expect that for any position of disadvantage there is a determinate oppressor or exploiter group. Precisely this lack of a personal direct antagonist, precisely the structural patterning of economic, social and cultural power, have a critical consequence. If disadvantage and deprivation cannot be redressed by direct recompense on the part of the individual or group responsible for injury, then we need other mechanisms for redistribution and inclusion. That is, principles of justice might be partly the upshot of ethical reasoning, but their motivation and their application are political matters. Once again, there are implications for education. In particular the discussion of what justice should entail is hardly separable from the question of how justice can be secured. And this question requires that citizens attend to the peculiar logic of politics, the interaction of political power with social, cultural, personal and economic power in their society, and the particular nature of political values.

## Conclusion

Young's theory of politics repays consideration by those engaged in education for citizenship or political education. This theory and others make the project of political education both more difficult and easier. More difficult because politics cannot be communicated just in terms of constitutions and given institutional structures for legislation, administration and accountability. Neither can it be communicated simply as that set of social and governing institutions that will promote justice. The problem with both of these approaches is that they are simply not equal to all the indeterminacies and tensions of politics. Glossing over, denying, or deferring discussion of these indeterminacies and tensions is not a practical pedagogical option for the simple reason that they are actually glaringly obvious to anyone who participates or watches politics, so the pretence that they don't exist invites sceptical and cynical responses.

On the other hand, this is not to pretend that education can be a matter of the brutal communication of the 'unvarnished truth'. Again, this is a distressingly common strategy from those adults who pretend that the important thing is to teach to young people that 'the world isn't fair', or that 'equality is a nice idea but not one we can ever attain' or other such simple minded, fatalistic and simply false nostrums ...

The trick with 'teaching politics' must be to enable people to focus on the ways in which political power is a power we can all participate in if and only if publicity and justice operate. It is a virtue of Iris Young's theory of politics that it addresses the power of politics.

## Acknowledgements

I am most grateful to Cissie Fu, Tim Markham and James Panton for very helpful responses to an earlier draft of this paper.

## References

Frazer, E. (ed.) (1999) *Political Education: special issue. Oxford Review of Education*, 25.

Frazer, E. (2000) Citizenship Education: anti-political culture and political education in Britain, *Political Studies*, 48, pp. 88–103.

Philp, M. (1997) Defining Political Corruption, *Political Studies*, 45, pp. 436–62.

Pring, R. (1999) Political Education: relevance of the humanities, in: E. Frazer (ed.) 1999, pp. 71–88.

Torney-Purta, J., J. Schwille and J. Amadeo (eds) (1999) *Civic Education Across Countries: twenty four national case studies from the IEA Civic Education Project* (Delft, Eburon Publishers).

Young, I. M. (1990a) *Justice and the Politics of Difference* (New Jersey, Princeton University Press).

Young, I. M. (1990b) *Throwing Like a Girl and other essays in feminist philosophy and social theory* (Bloomington IA, Indiana University Press).

Young, I. M. (1995) Together in Difference: transforming the logic of group political conflict, in: W. Kymlicka (ed.) *The Rights of Minority Cultures* (Oxford, Oxford University Press).

Young, I. M. (1997) *Intersecting Voices: dilemmas of gender, political philosophy and policy* (Princeton NJ, Princeton University Press).

Young, I. M. (2000) *Inclusion and Democracy* (Oxford, Oxford University Press).

# 4

# Democracy, Social Justice and Education: Feminist strategies in a globalising world

PENNY ENSLIN

*University of the Witwatersrand*

## I

The work of Iris Marion Young counts among the most significant contributions to normative political theory in recent years, especially for those with an interest in feminist political theory. Although education is not among Young's central concerns, she does comment on educational issues from time to time (Sardoc & Shaughnessy, 2001). Yet her contribution to contemporary political philosophy is rich in analysis and argument of significance for philosophers of education and the issues they address. My interest in this paper is in Young's views on democracy and social justice, and their implications for education under conditions of growing global inequality.

I will not try here to do anything like full justice to the many ways in which Young's work illuminates the challenges of educating for democracy and what is for me the related feminist project in education, but will address these in so far as they focus on a central question: given her commitment to both social justice and to recognition of the political and ethical significance of difference, to what extent does Young's position allow for transnational interventions in education to foster democracy?

In taking up this question this paper comprises the following stages. I start by exploring some of Iris Young's arguments on the relationship between democracy and social justice with particular reference to their implications for education. Then, I argue that if Young's ideas on democracy and social justice are extended to the issue of global justice, the strategies for global feminist intervention which she offers should be extended, at least when it comes to educational intervention, to allow for a wider range of actions in support of global justice through education for democracy than Young's work so far seems to allow.

I write from the perspective of Southern Africa, noting that Iris Young herself is careful to stress the importance of context. Young emphasises (Young, 2000, p. 15) that although she writes primarily for and about the United States, she tries to contribute to the thinking of those addressing similar issues elsewhere, saying that she hopes that her reflections 'may fruitfully contribute to the thinking of those concerned to further democratic practices anywhere in the world'. And so they do, prompting precisely the kind of stimulus to conversation that Young sets out to provoke.

## II

In Iris Young's political theory democracy and justice are closely related. Breaking with the tradition that interprets justice in terms of the distribution of material goods and social positions, in *Justice and the Politics of Difference* she challenges the distributive paradigm, arguing that 'social justice means the elimination of institutionalised domination and oppression' (Young, 1990, p. 15). In this book, 'The idea of justice ... shifts from a focus on distributive patterns to procedural issues of participation in deliberation and decision making' (Young, 1990, p. 34). The wider scope of justice includes having the power to make decisions, the division of labour (the allocation of jobs and how they are defined) and culture (the meanings attributed to people from different groups). Justice becomes relational rather than static, and is concerned with action and process. Hence Young's interest in oppression and domination as the social conditions that are definitive of injustice and act as the institutional constraints on self-development and self-determination respectively (1990, p. 37). She describes self-development as 'developing and exercising one's capacities and expressing one's experience', and self-determination as 'participating in determining one's action and the conditions of one's action' (1990, p. 37).

This approach to justice has clear relevance to justice in education. Just as Young leaves appropriate space for the relevance of distribution of resources, so the first and most obvious issue in considering social justice in education is the distribution of resources, as Young acknowledges (1990, p. 26). The unequal distribution of funds for school buildings and facilities, teacher education and salaries, and learning materials is an acknowledged marker of unequal access and outcomes in education for different social classes, boys and girls, and ethnic and cultural groups. But Young's theory of justice also points to the need to view justice in education in broader terms. Reflecting the effects of structural inequalities outside the school on educational opportunities within, injustice may also be the consequence of lower expectations of achievement towards girls or working class and black children, and for me also of traditions within groups, e.g. that girls need less education than boys, or as in Lesotho that boys will inevitably receive less schooling because of their herding duties and their adult destiny as migrant labourers.

But shifting to Young's focus on social justice as the removal of institutionalised domination and oppression brings to the fore the importance of education in the promotion of social justice through extending to all the opportunity and capacity for self-development and self-determination, by critically addressing the role of schooling in the division of labour, in determining who gets to make decisions, and in the oppressive meanings given to cultural difference. When it comes to educating for self-determination, Young's contribution to deliberative theories of democracy is of considerable significance, highlighting the importance of acquisition of capabilities not only for work and political participation, but also for self-development and participation in the life of the community (see Sardoc & Shaughnessy, 2001, p. 98).

While not rejecting the deliberative model of democracy, Young (1996, 2000) sees the usual accounts of this model of democracy as focusing too narrowly on critical argument. Her conception of deliberation goes beyond the forms of critical argument that favour male, white, middle-class participants, to a broadened, communicative theory of deliberation that accommodates an expanded set of discursive interactions, through greeting (or recognition that lubricates discussion), rhetoric (attracting and maintaining each others' attention), and storytelling (conveying the experiences of differently situated people). Such narratives, the most important of the three forms of communication, provide not only a way of sharing experiences and informing groups about each other's values and cultures. They also have a crucial epistemic function, conveying situated knowledge that provides a collective social wisdom that includes all positions and showing need and justified entitlement in developing policy, solving problems and making decisions. Thus group difference becomes a 'deliberative resource'. And democratic practice, in turn, is an element of social justice and a means for its promotion. Deliberative processes promote just policies because: 'If all significantly affected by problems and their solutions are included in the discussion and decision-making on the basis of equality and non-domination, and if they interact reasonably and constitute a public where people are accountable to one another, then the results of their discussion is likely to be the most wise and just' (Young, 2000, pp. 29–30). Deliberative democracy creates the epistemic conditions for arriving at proposals likely to effect wise results, based on judgements that are both normatively correct and empirically sound. Furthermore, communicative democracy makes possible the transformation of citizens' opinions and desires, moving them from a partial, subjective understanding of the issues to an enlarged, objective view in which the interests of all are taken into account.

Although Young sees being reasonable—being willing to listen to others and to have them influence one's opinions, to explain one's claims to them with the aim of winning their agreement—as a capacity that does not require special training, her theory of communicative democracy and its relationship with justice has considerable implications for the education of democratic citizens. While we may all have the capacity to be reasonable (Young, 2000, p. 38), there is much that educative schooling can do to develop deliberative skills (see Enslin, Pendlebury & Tjiattas, 2001), whether as critical argument or in the more diverse styles of communicative democracy. Especially in schools that include a diversity of learners, skills of listening across difference can be practised in a range of curriculum activities, from literatures that embrace a variety of written and verbal styles to the arts and especially history that goes beyond the local and the national. Across the curriculum there is enormous scope for teaching critical evaluation not only of arguments, but also of greeting, rhetoric and storytelling, asking: 'Is this discourse respectful, publicly assertable, and does it stand up to public challenge? The only cure for false, manipulative, or inappropriate talk is more talk that exposes or corrects it, whether as a string of reasons, a mode of recognition, a way of making points, or a narrative (Young, 2000, p. 79).

In turning next to a consideration of democracy as an element and a condition of *global* justice, I am going to suggest that Young's defence of the close continuity between democracy and social justice, together with the educational implications of this connection, should be applied globally.


## III

If pursuing the goal of social justice requires not only that domination and oppression in their various forms be alleviated but also that democracy be pursued as 'both an element and a condition of social justice' (Young, 1990, p. 67), with the implications for education explored so far, what does all this imply for the global pursuit of democracy? Relatedly, what does it suggest about the education of democratic citizens in a global context?

In her concluding chapters to both *Justice and the Politics of Difference* (1990) and *Democracy and Inclusion* (2000) Young reflects on the international or global implications of the discussion in preceding chapters. While pointing out the historical and social situatedness of her critical theory in Western capitalist societies like the USA, Young regards her ideas as relevant to societies in the Southern or Eastern hemispheres. Subject to modifications to meet differences in context, she rightly sees her work as having some global applicability to issues of social justice within nations and between them (1990, p. 257). But, noting that contextually varying forms of domination and oppression occur in all contexts, Young's comments on global social justice focus mainly on questions of international justice *between* countries. She points out not only the privileged position of the USA compared with the degree of oppression in the rest of the world, but also that its state and private institutions contribute to oppression in other societies (1990, p. 257). Distributive injustice is evident in the huge inequities between living standards in industrialised Western societies and much of the rest of the world, because of the effects of colonialism, unequal resources and prevailing inequities in global investment, trade and finance. For my purposes it is important to deliberative democracy as a goal that huge discrepancies in educational resources between rich and poor countries are also a distributive injustice with consequences beyond access to educative schooling. Global injustice in education also takes a non-distributive form. As Young argues, viewed non-distributively, global injustice is also marked by cultural inequalities and the division of labour. 'Multinational corporations, trade agreements, financial institutions such as the International Monetary Fund exercise significant power to influence the policies of many states in ways that often make ordinary working and poor people worse off' (Young, 2000, p. 188).

Given these features of global injustice, Young disagrees with those who view justice as an obligation only to co-nationals, taking the view that relations of justice are present whenever people are connected by commercial, political or communications institutions (Young, 2000, p. 246). She extends to the pursuit of justice her emphasis on the significance of social groups, arguing that oppressed groups should be given similar specific representation internationally to that she proposes domestically. 'To the extent that the well-being of individuals partly depends on the flourishing of the meanings and practices that serve as the sources of their selves, then those people should have the means collectively to decide how to maintain and promote their flourishing as a people' (2000, p. 256).

But Young rejects a nationalist solution to the demand for self-development of distinct peoples. Although she recognises that group distinctiveness is often connected to particular places and resources, she opposes a conception of self-development cast in terms of control over a bounded, contiguous territory (2000, p. 261). 'In her more complex account of self-determination as non-domination, self-determination is defined in terms of peoples having governance institutions of their own within which they make decisions on their goals, as well as in interpreting their way of life' (2000, p. 259), but in relation with others who may be affected by their actions.

Young emphasises that relational autonomy, which she proposes should be applied to small ethnic or indigenous groups and to nation states, should be interpreted in a way that shifts its interpretation 'away from independence towards autonomy in the context of interdependent relations among peoples' (2000, p. 258). Drawing on Pettit's work (1997), she proposes an understanding of freedom as *non-domination* rather than as non-interference. Significantly for my concerns in this paper, Young takes the position that there is sometimes a need for measures that 'interfere with actions in order to restrict dominative power and promote co-operation. Interference is not arbitrary if its purpose is to minimise domination, and if it is done in a way that takes the interests and voices of affected parties into account' (Young, 2000, p. 259). So, instead of endorsing a traditional conception of sovereignty, Young limits the rights of nation states in the interests of allowing outsiders to interfere against 'dominative harm' or to promote co-operative relationships and collective action. But she qualifies this by emphasising that self-determination implies 'a presumption of non-interference' (2000, p. 265).

I will return presently to the conditions under which interference might be called for. But first we should note that Young's proposed institutions for pursuing global justice are quite modest, apparently designed to focus mainly on promoting self-determination of peoples. So she notes, for example, the emergence, outside of formal state institutions, of international civil society involved in the development of a global public life, e.g. in women's movements, the peace movement and economic networks like those campaigning for the cancellation of third world debt, as well as those pursuing global democracy.

In addition to the growth of international civil society, Young points as a second sphere for the development of global democracy to the development of global institutions of governance. These institutions should govern relations between the world's peoples, accommodating their claims for self-determination through local autonomy. They would include global institutions tasked with the role of protecting human rights, with policies formulated by involving all peoples concerned. Where interventions to respond to human rights abuses are required, they should carry international sanction. Global institutions of governance should be democratically organised and should also counter the domination that private bodies, including multinational corporations, wield over poor peoples. Organisations that regulate intergovernmental and extra governmental interaction, like the European Union and the UN Security Council, could be more democratically structured, and those like the World Trade Organisation and the International Monetary Fund are also not open to scrutiny or accountable to those affected by their policies. In addition to reducing the undemocratic presence of such bodies, Young proposes that a reformed UN could provide a stronger means of regulating global interactions, e.g. through a restructured Security Council and possibly the addition of a directly elected People's Assembly (Young, 2000, p. 273).

I assume that the institutions to which Young points as means of fostering global justice—both those of international civil society and global institutions of governance—must, if they reflect democracy's role as a condition and a component of justice, be deliberative forums. Through a range of discursive interactions, conveying the situated knowledge of those differently placed across the globe, in such a way that reasonable interaction leads to wise decisions that are the product of an enlarged and objective view of all claims to justice. But what, given that Young allows for interference to prevent dominative harm, of those states in which democracy is constrained, or barely present at all? This seems to pose a problem for Young's stipulation that 'the self-determination of peoples requires that the peoples have the right to participate in designing and implementing intergovernmental institutions aimed at minimising domination' (2000, p. 265). Even if a way is found for the world's peoples to be represented in structures of global governance other than through their governments, it seems to me that people living in contexts where democratic practice is limited by their own governments, and possibly other institutions too, may even be restricted in their opportunities to participate in international civil society. I base this observation partly on the assumption that democracy works best when it is an established habit, where citizens are used to its exercise as a matter of course. But I do not mean this to imply that persons living in undemocratic conditions are incapable of deliberation and other forms of conduct appropriate to democratic processes. Mine is more a claim about the optimal conditions under which democracy—and also justice—can flourish. This claim seems especially pertinent to the development of international institutions of democracy and social justice in which there is a danger that participants from states in which democratic practices are well established and routine can dominate deliberation between groups whose interests are at stake by the mere fact of being at home in deliberative conditions, however diverse the forms of deliberation in which they engage.

Globalisation without the development of equal capacities among the world's peoples to resist and work with it will surely exacerbate its now painfully apparent accompanying inequalities. But Young opposes intervention to foster democracy in particular societies. While outsiders may require, on moral grounds, equal respect for all individuals' basic rights, she argues that they should not impose a particular interpretation of democracy on them. While ideally self-governing peoples should be governed democratically, others may not go further than fostering a global or regional context that facilitates the establishment and maintenance of democracy (Young, 2000, p. 264). Perhaps much depends on the distinction between requiring and encouraging, but it is significant that Young limits interference to this extent while acknowledging that 'One rarely finds a set of interests agreed upon by all members of a group for guiding their autonomous government. Too often moreover, some members of the group stand in relations of structural inequality or domination over other members of the group. Under these circumstances, promoting self-determination of the group may further the domination of some of its members' (2000, p. 263). If Young concedes the point that domination is present within groups, why does she place such strict limits on intervention?

The problem of intra group domination is compounded by the associated difficulty that the dominant members can eschew reasonableness and use their position of dominance to further their own interests, undermining the conditions required for deliberation and hence for social justice. The conduct of the dominant, as they work to protect their interests through power over the definition and membership of groups, can include one strategy of which Young is aware, which is the use of the ideal of universal citizenship outside western capitalist societies to determine the norm of citizenship so as to reproduce the privileges of the dominant.

Setting aside states whose leaders do not even pretend to support democracy, even allowing for some local variation to match local custom, democracy must surely have some basic unvarying features that are desirable in all contexts. These include a constitution with some separation of powers and protection of human rights. Regular free and fair elections, crudely aggregative though they are, are a means of expressing the general will of the people, at least to the extent that they offer the opportunity to evict governments whose record suggests to the electorate that they would be better off taking their chances with an alternative party or group vying openly and fairly for the opportunity to govern. This requires that citizens see themselves as having the right and the opportunity to evaluate the performance of their government and the extent to which it serves the needs and wider aspirations of its citizens. Without some such conditions being met, it is unlikely that the members of a society will be able to engage in forms of deliberation that are necessary conditions for that society to be said to be self-determining, developing and implementing institutions that minimise domination within that society as Young requires, rather than being dominated from within. Democracy and a degree of individual autonomy seem to be mutually dependent goods.

My claim is that all people globally need education to successfully engage with and resist globalisation as well as to influence decisions in their own communities; the two are related. This posits a serious obstacle to global justice, given that one key feature of global inequality is educational inequality. This inequality is partly manifested in inequities in access to at least those kinds of individual autonomy that enable a citizen to be sufficiently in charge of her life to allow her to resist domination and oppression, to be among those on whose consent those who put themselves forward as leaders are dependent for their legitimacy. There are at least some minimal elements of autonomy required to participate meaningfully in democratic processes. These include the possibility of having an opinion of one's own, of disagreeing with one's peers as well as with those in authority. One may have good reason from time to time to revise one's opinions in the light of new evidence, or a different interpretation of the old evidence, and one may speak rather than be required to be silent, as women still are in many communities. There are regimes that stand on their own sovereignty in relation to other states while not demonstrating much interest in whether they have the autonomous consent of the citizens they purport to represent, or in providing schooling that encourages the capacity for individual autonomy.

These considerations imply that some forms of global educational intervention, both within and beyond the distributive model of justice, are a prerequisite for the promotion of global democracy and social justice.

## IV

Given the qualified support that Iris Young offers for interference, on what kinds of issues should we contemplate global regulation? She has proposed seven regulatory regimes which would present 'a thin set of general rules' in terms of which governments, organisations and individuals would pursue global co-operation and justice, though leaving open the exact number of such regimes as well as how their jurisdiction would be defined: '(1) peace and security, (2) environment, (3) trade and finance, (4) direct investment and capital utilization, (5) communications and transportation, (6) human rights, including labour standards and welfare rights, (7) citizenship and migration' (Young, 2000, p. 267). Acknowledging that Young leaves some room for interpretation of this list and its scope, it is quite a modest proposal. It does not explicitly include education, though on some interpretation of 'rights' education could be included in the sixth category. So could intervention on behalf of women, though the list does not include transnational regulation of the status and role of women. Some feminists, myself included, would argue that it should.

More recently, Young (2002) has spelt out further her views on what forms of transnational feminist activism are appropriate, in her critical response to appeals to women's liberation made in attempts to justify the invasion of Afghanistan and the then threatened invasion of Iraq on the grounds that it would have the benefit of freeing Afghan and Iraqi women from oppression. 'Some expressions of concern for women's rights function to legitimate Western domination of non-Western others' (2002, p. 4), and exhibit assumptions about Western superiority. Young sees certain feminist arguments as associated with such discourse, particularly those of Susan Okin (1999) who Young sees as creating two opposed positions: a universal liberal commitment to freedom and equality on the one hand and on the other multiculturalist support for preserving cultural practices, with individual freedom trumping the freedom of communities to maintain their traditions. This dichotomy, for Young, creates a hierarchy in which the universal is favoured over the particular, thus legitimating domination. But while she opposes forms of feminism that she sees as legitimating domination by appealing to universal rights, Young does (2002) allow for some feminist advocacy and suggests conditions under which feminists can engage without succumbing to western chauvinism. This seems to extend her earlier position on what degree of interference is justifiable.

Avoiding the tendencies of liberal Western feminists that she rejects does not, for Young, preclude their protesting and trying to alleviate women's oppression. She proposes four strategies for doing so. In considering them, we can reflect on how they might relate educatively to the project of developing global democracy, explored earlier. The first three of these focus on actions that western feminists should undertake in their own countries, beginning with drawing attention to widespread unjust practices accepted as normal, such as rape, abuse and exploitation of women. Young also urges the need to find similarities in the condition of women, instead of emphasising differences. She warns against concentrating attention on practices that repel western women. In seeking similarities we will be less likely to ignore the indecencies in western societies. So, for example, denouncing dowry murder has to be accompanied by ongoing attention to the incidence of murder of American women by men with guns. Western women's acceptance of images of beauty that lead them to undergo cosmetic surgery should accompany calling attention to genital surgeries. Third, if feminists call for a right to exit from restrictive cultural communities, they should also oppose state practices that make exit difficult, like immigration regulations that make exit from oppressive conditions difficult for legal and illegal immigrant women.

It is Young's fourth suggestion that most interests me. This is that for feminist engagement that both promotes justice and is respectful we should 'find and support women and men within each society and community who themselves criticise domination and oppression and are working for change' (Young, 2002, p. 12). Without focusing on any particular group, such action should involve facilitating debate with and among different groups and listening to them, as well as supporting their self-organisation.

Each of these strategies can be taken up educationally. Drawing attention to unjust practices everywhere and to the similarities in how women are placed across societies can be best taken up through literature that emphasises not only diversity but also similarity. Recognising that oppression affects girls in all societies, though in differing ways, international teacher organisations can cooperate in responding to nutritional problems among girls in poor countries as well as eating disorders among affluent girls. Across most societies there is a common need to counter the cultural hegemony exercised by the export of some of the worst elements of American culture across the globe, e.g. through trashy teen movies. Facilitating exit from oppressive conditions also has an educational dimension, calling for education to ensure that women can obtain employment if the conditions created for them by the decision to exit so require. But all of these possibilities take us back ultimately to the requirement that education everywhere should provide girls with opportunities to develop a capacity for autonomy.

Pursuing these strategies and goals under conditions of global interdependence leads me to conclude by suggesting two directions in which Young's feminist strategies should be extended, recognising her observation that: 'Responsibility for promoting global justice ... falls more heavily on those whose actions more profoundly affect the condition of the actions of others' (2000, p. 250).

## V

The improved health of democracy in the most powerful countries can and should benefit democracy elsewhere. Indeed feminists in the most powerful countries can be said to have a duty to be politically active, given the scope and influence of their countries' political order in the wider world.

First, I suggest a strategy that is consistent with those proposed by Young, which is that western feminists seeking to promote global justice should engage in activism within their own societies. This could take the form, for example, of supporting and extending campaigns for fair trade that try to ensure that producers of agricultural and craft products in developing countries receive a fair price for their goods, or supporting debt cancellation for poor countries burdened with debt that hampers development, including schooling, and whose women carry a heavy burden of poverty.

While I acknowledge with Young that the political clout of women is limited in all countries, even in the USA, such activists might seek to influence their governments' foreign policies by campaigning for increased but democratically negotiated and deployed foreign aid, which if sufficient could be the start of genuine redistribution of financial and other resources from rich to poor countries. Other possible campaigns could demand earmarking of some of these funds for spending on girls and women, with a meaningful role for them in decisions on expenditure and local management of the funds. Another possible area of activism within rich countries is to support campaigns for growing awareness in those countries of the unacceptable power wielded domestically and internationally by multinational corporations, whose headquarters are located in those countries, whose laws have the best chance of getting to grips with the corporations' excessive freedom from accountability. Successful political campaigns of this kind in rich countries could have the additional benefit of reducing their undemocratic influence over polities and economies in poor countries whose weaker legal infrastructure and civil society makes them more vulnerable to the actions of corporations than those in richer countries whose resources are greater all round. This would require that women in rich countries, as voters and consumers, pay greater attention to foreign policy issues than they have done to date. There is some evidence that this is taking place already in the network of movements opposing globalisation and some of its effects, though some such groups are inclined to protect their own economic interests against those of others.

My second proposal is that western feminists should actively promote education for democracy in societies where it has a more tenuous foothold than in western democracies. In making this suggestion I do not doubt that there is much that can be done domestically in all countries to address problems of social injustice and the associated imperfections of all democracies. But my point is that promoting democracy and social justice globally is a project that needs to recognise the interrelatedness of all countries in this endeavour, as well as the imbalances in their resources. Western feminists and their governments should contribute resources and influence to promote schooling in poor countries. This can be done in ways that are true to Young's stipulation that interference is permissible if undertaken against dominative harm. Without an drastic expansion of the kind of intervention modestly exemplified by the work of NGOs like the Cambridge Female Education Trust, which promotes girls' education in Zimbabwe through improved access to schooling for girls and supporting female teachers (see Ansell, 2002), I fear that the possibilities for achieving global democracy and social justice are slight.

## References

Ansell, N. (2002) Secondary Education Reform in Lesotho and Zimbabwe and the Needs of Rural Girls: pronouncements, policy and practice, *Comparative Education*, 38:1.

Enslin, P., Pendlebury, S. & Tjiattas, M. (2001) Deliberative Democracy, Diversity and the Challenges of Citizenship Education, *Journal of Philosophy of Education*, 35:1.

Okin, S. M. (1999) Is Multiculturalism Bad for Women?, in: K. Cohen, M. Howard & M. Nussbaum (eds), *Is Multiculturalism Bad for Women?* (Princeton NJ, Princeton University Press).

Sardoc, M. & Shaughnessy, M. (2001) An Interview with Iris Marion Young, *Educational Philosophy and Theory*, 33:1.

Young, I. M. (1990) *Justice and the Politics of Difference* (Princeton NJ, Princeton University Press).

Young, I. M. (1996) Communication and the Other, in: S. Benhabib (ed.), *Democracy and Difference* (Princeton NJ, Princeton University Press).

Young, I. M. (2000) *Inclusion and Democracy* (Oxford, Oxford University Press).

Young, I. M. (2002) The Rhetoric of Women's Rights in the 'War on Terrorism', Paper presented to Metropolis 2002 Conference, Sept 10, Oslo.

## 5

# Towards a Contextualized Analysis of Social Justice in Education[1]

SHARON GEWIRTZ

*Centre for Public Policy Research, King's College London*

### Introduction

What criteria can we use to judge whether an educational policy or practice is socially just? How do we make comparative assessments of social justice in education? In other words, how can we tell whether one national or local education system or one educational institution or one educational policy or practice is more socially just than another? In this paper I want to demonstrate how Iris Marion Young's thinking on justice can help us to answer these questions. In particular, I want to draw on her insights about the multi-dimensional nature of justice and her emphasis on the way in which social in/justice is expressed in mundane, institutional and face-to-face interactions.

In the paper I am not going to attempt to give some kind of definitive, abstract conceptualisation of what should count as justice in education against which educational systems, institutions, policies and practices can then be judged. Rather what I want to do is to argue that it is not possible to resolve the question of what counts as justice in education at a purely abstract level, and that what counts as justice can only properly be understood within specific contexts of interpretation and enactment. There are three interlocking reasons for this need to contextualize judgements about social justice that I want to illustrate and discuss. The first reason relates to the *multi-dimensional* nature of justice at an abstract level. In other words, as Young's (1990) work shows us, justice can mean many things simultaneously and, as Nancy Fraser (1997) has argued in her critical development of Young's work, some of these things are unavoidably in tension with one another. Therefore in practice, I would want to argue, it is unrealistic—or utopian—to imagine that we can pursue policies and practices that are 'purely' just. In practice, pursuing certain dimensions of social justice will inevitably mean neglecting, or sacrificing, others. Hence, any meaningful discussion of what counts as justice needs to engage with concrete, practical dilemmas and not merely abstract conceptualisations.

The second reason why we can only properly understand social justice within its contexts of realisation is that justice concerns are always in practice likely to be mediated by other kinds of concerns that motivate actors. There are two kinds of concerns I am thinking of in particular here—a) other norms that are not concerned with justice but which might in practice compete or conflict with justice concerns;

and b) constraints over which agents have little or no control, for example, dominant discourses or power relations, or legal or economic constraints. Therefore we need to recognize *the mediated nature of just practices.*

Finally, the value we place on different conceptions of justice and how we respond to contradictions between different conceptions or to constraints on just practices will be shaped to a significant degree by the level and setting at which we are operating. So what counts as justice is *level- and context-dependent.* For example, the relevant justice issues or criteria may be different, be mediated differently and therefore need to be dealt with differently from the different vantage points of policy makers, managers, teachers or social workers. Furthermore, *within* each of these occupational groups there will be differences in terms of what is possible and/or desirable according to different national, regional, and/or local contexts.

In the rest of the paper I want to use a concrete example to illustrate these points—and, in doing so, the value of an analytic approach, which builds upon Young's formulation of justice, that focuses on different dimensions of justice and the conflicts between them, and on the mediated nature and level- and context-dependency of just practices in education. The example I want to use is the case of Martin, age 15, and his mother Mrs. Miles. Mrs. Miles was one of a number of mothers interviewed as part of a project I have recently been involved in looking at the origins and implementation of an English government initiative which was designed to tackle social exclusion and raise standards of education in schools in areas of disadvantage.[2]

Mrs. Miles and her son Martin live in a council flat in Wellford, a mainly white seaside English town with pockets of high unemployment, low income, poor housing, health and environmental conditions and high recorded levels of crime. Mrs. Miles is a white lone mother with two sons of 'mixed race'. Only Martin, the younger son, still lives at home. Mrs. Miles left school herself at sixteen with no qualifications. However, she has since attended courses at her local further education college in counselling, reflexology, aromatherapy and massage. She is not in paid employment so money is tight, but Mrs. Miles does voluntary work for a domestic violence organization—she is herself a survivor of domestic violence—and she also does voluntary work for an organization that supports people with drug addiction problems.

Martin is considered to be disruptive at school and, as a consequence of his challenging behaviour, he was temporarily excluded from his secondary school four times in one year before being permanently excluded at the age of 11. Following this he was out of the school system for nearly two years because no other school would accept him. He is now at college but has missed out on his GCSEs because he has missed so much school. Although, according to Mrs. Miles, Martin is 'a wonderful football player' and 'very athletic, it is all gone by the wayside now. He is going in the wrong direction ... going down the drug [route], in and out of court' and Mrs. Miles, who makes valiant efforts (including giving up college herself) to, as she puts it, 'pull him back', feels 'powerless to what path he is going to walk down'.

In what follows I will use extracts from our interview with Mrs. Miles which tell her story of a largely unsuccessful attempt in the face of a seemingly unresponsive educational system to get her son access to the kind of help and education she feels he needs. I will then use this story to demonstrate the importance and value of an approach to the conceptualisation of social justice which pays attention to its multi-dimensional and conflictual nature, the mediated nature of just practices and the need to be sensitive to the different contexts and levels in which just practices may be enacted.

## Mrs. Miles' Story

As I have already mentioned, Mrs. Miles was interviewed as part of a study of an English education policy designed to tackle social exclusion. Her story was one of a number of depressing tales relayed to us by mothers of children with challenging behaviour. These were tales of mothers' struggles to be heard by what felt to them to be a predominantly unyielding, inflexible and uncompassionate educational system.

I want to begin with an extended extract from Mrs. Miles' interview which captures key aspects of her struggle with the authorities and the remarkable degree of determination with which she has tried to get her voice heard and her son's interests attended to:

> I thought the [secondary] school focused on Martin's bad behaviour too much. I thought they didn't make allowances, because once they found that Martin is a difficult child—I am not saying he is not—they already knew this from the past [primary] school, it had already started in the last year or so in the past school. We brought in a child psychologist, because I had picked it up straight away that there was something wrong, so I went looking for help, because I knew what was going to happen, I could see it so clearly. And in the first year at [the secondary school] we brought in another child psychologist who said Martin did not have emotional problems and I disagreed. Then the case was basically closed and it carried on ...

> He went through five stages, five exclusions almost until it becomes permanent ... I said let's bring in a child psychologist here, let's find out what's happening here. The school brought another child psychologist in. We were supposed to meet him on a weekly basis but it only seemed to happen once or twice. I seemed to have more insight than any of those child psychologists. He was eventually sent to a system that they had in the school ... Learning Difficulty Centre, I think, a separate part of the school, full of computers, and if Martin got too difficult in a class he would be sent out to the room and it was OK, it wasn't too bad. Then he ended up in there more than he was in class. He would be taken out in there, taken and put in there. Then eventually we had this thing drawn up that he would spend more time in there than in class, but at the same time while he was in there he was missing out his education, because he wasn't getting ... what he needed in there. It was more about his behaviour than his education because his behaviour was obviously difficult ... He eventually got excluded full time so he no longer went to school ... They wanted to give

him tuition for an hour a day and I said, no I wanted it looked into more … I want to know why he behaves like that, I want more people brought in, I need some help here, Martin needs some support, and this is when we got the child psychologist in, we got sent to a psychiatrist. … All these people got together to evaluate Martin as a person, and they did a few tests with the child psychologist with numbers, because what happened was the child psychologist said this kid might be dyslexic. If he is then great, we have got somewhere, because at one point the evaluation was that Martin disturbed the class when he struggled with not knowing the answers. That was picked up along the way but it was overlooked at the same time … I thought that was really valid. I thought, wow that would make sense. Martin is starting to misbehave as soon as he realizes he can't do it …

So it was kind of looking like we were getting somewhere, but we never really got anywhere even though he was statemented … I went to see our local MP, I went to see him twice and it went straight over his head.

The end result was that no other school would take him. Whenever we got near a school they started to do a risk assessment and they said that he would be at risk to their school because he had behaviour statements on him and everything, stuff like that. In the end I sent him to [an out-of-school support unit] which is an hour or two a day, culminating in six or eight hours a week, even though I didn't want to. I was trying to hold out because it wasn't enough … I had been to meeting after meeting. At one point I thought I was being heard, then it fell apart again. Then eventually they offered [a college place] … so although I wasn't happy with it because he was in a college and he was only fourteen and he was with children a year older than him … but it meant more time, more structured—because by this time he was off the rails, he is in and out of courts, he is in trouble with the police …

Asked about whether she feels that the school valued her views, Mrs. Miles is critical of where the school draws the boundaries of what constitutes an acceptable expression of parental view:

Mrs. Miles: I am quite good at expressing myself and getting my point across.
Interviewer: Are they happy for you to do that?
Mrs. Miles: Well it depends. If I go in and say, well hold on a minute, your teacher might have been having a bad day and taken it out on my son, because my son has gone home and told me that the teacher has said, 'Why haven't you got school shoes on?' and he has gone, 'because I haven't got any' and she has actually shamed him. Where do you draw the line between your teacher having a bad day and taking it out on my son, and my son having a bad day and taking it out on your teacher? We aren't allowed to go to that area, because the teachers are right and the teachers are perfect, and after all Martin is just a little boy. So if you are on side and saying what they want to hear you are fine.

Mrs. Miles also suspects that classism, racism and assumptions about what comprises a 'proper' family also played a part in denying her child access to what she sees as adequate levels and appropriate kinds of provision:

> I think that people are prejudiced, and I hope this does not come across as being a real victim statement, but I believe that if I lived in a big house with more money then maybe we would have stood a better chance, and I spoke a bit better and I had a husband, and I had more support, and Martin wasn't mixed race then maybe Martin may have been helped a bit more, considered a bit more.

As part of the government initiative we were studying, some schools had set up parent education projects to help build 'social capital' in the 'disadvantaged' communities the schools were meant to be serving. However, according to Mrs. Miles, it was the teachers not the parents who needed educating about how better to relate to others:

> I think the teachers could do with a bit more awareness of how to integrate with other parents, I suppose they only live what they live and only know what they know, and are brought up with what they are brought up with, so maybe something for them, something like a course for them to deal with, I don't know ...

So let me now use this story to illustrate the key points about conceptualizing and evaluating justice that I set out at the beginning of the paper.

### The Multi-dimensional Nature of Justice

First, the story brings out a whole range of forms of injustice that Mrs. Miles and her son may have experienced,[3] which help to illustrate the multi-dimensional nature of social justice. There are a number of ways of categorizing justice and capturing its multi-dimensionality, but for present purposes I will use the three-fold categorization I have used elsewhere (e.g. Cribb and Gewirtz, 2003) that builds on the work of Young (1990) as well as that of Nancy Fraser (1997). The three categories are distributive, recognitional and associational justice.

Distributive justice refers to the principles by which goods are distributed in society. This is the conventional conception of justice, defined by Rawls (1972, p. 7) as concerning 'the way in which the major social institutions ... distribute fundamental rights and duties and determine the distribution of advantages from social co-operation'. Distributive justice includes concerns about what Fraser (1997, pp. 13–14) calls economic justice. This is defined as the absence of exploitation, marginalization and material deprivation. Young defines exploitation as the 'oppression [that] occurs through a steady process of the transfer of the results of the labor of one social group to benefit another' and marginalization as expulsion 'from useful participation in social life'. Marginalization, Young says, can also result in subjection 'to severe material deprivation and even extermination' (Young, 1990, pp. 49, 53). However, distributive justice can also include concerns about the distribution of cultural and social resources (or in Bourdieuan terms cultural and social capital).[4]

The second form of justice, recognitional justice refers to the absence of cultural domination, non-recognition and disrespect (Fraser, 1997, p. 14) associated with what Young calls cultural imperialism. As Young puts it:

> To experience cultural imperialism means to experience how the dominant meanings of a society render the particular perspective of one's own group invisible at the same time as they stereotype one's group and mark it out as Other.

> Cultural imperialism involves the universalization of a dominant group's experience and culture, and its establishment as the norm ... Often without noticing they do so, the dominant groups project their own experience as representative of humanity as such ...

> Those living under cultural imperialism find themselves defined from the outside, positioned, placed, by a network of dominant meanings they experience as arising from elsewhere, from those with whom they do not identify and who do not identify with them (Young, 1990, p. 59).

This conception of justice also draws on the work of Charles Taylor who has argued that recognition of and respect for people's cultures, ways of life and values is essential for their dignity, sense of worth and self esteem. As he puts it:

> our identity is partly shaped by recognition or its absence, often by the *mis*recognition of others, and so a person or group of people can suffer real damage, real distortion, if the people or society around them mirror back to them a confining or demeaning or contemptible picture of themselves.

> ... misrecognition shows not just a lack of due respect. It can inflict a grievous wound, saddling its victims with a crippling self-hatred. Due recognition is not just a courtesy we owe people. It is a vital human need (Taylor, 1992, pp. 25–6).

The third form of justice in this framework is associational. Associational justice can be defined by the absence of:

> Patterns of association amongst individuals and amongst groups which prevent some people from participating fully in decisions which affect the conditions within which they live and act (Power and Gewirtz, 2001, p. 41).

Although Young does not explicitly refer to associational justice, the form of justice that this label denotes is, for Young, a necessary precondition for other dimensions of justice as well as something to be valued in its own right. More specifically, Young is committed to democracy and group representation for the disadvantaged:

> Social justice entails democracy. Persons should be involved in collective discussion and decision-making in all the settings that depend on their commitment, action, and obedience to rules—workplaces, schools, neighborhoods, and so on. When such institutions privilege some groups over others, actual democracy requires group representation for the disadvantaged.

> Not only do just procedures require group representation in order to ensure that oppressed or disadvantaged groups have a voice, but such representation is also the best means to promote just outcomes of the deliberative process (Young, 1990, p. 191).

Each of these dimensions of justice—distributive, recognitional and associational—is exemplified in the story of the Mileses.

In terms of distributive justice, as a lone parent Mrs. Miles is disadvantaged by a set of economic and fiscal state policies which privilege paid over unpaid work (Land, 1999). Mrs. Miles works hard—battling for her son, working for two voluntary organizations, trying to get a formal education and gain qualifications herself (or to put it in cruder economic terms investing in herself as human capital). Her mothering work in particular takes up a huge amount of time, and the demands put on her by her son's college to be on permanent call should they not be able to cope with Martin have meant she has been unable to pursue her own college courses:

> any time of day they will ring you up and you have to go and get him. I suppose to them it is their last resort as they see it ... There have been times where I have said, 'I am not going to be around today, if you have trouble with him then it's OK to send him home but don't ring me', and they will do things like, this is nuts, they will let him out for a fag break every fifty minutes. Then they will ring me up and ask if he can watch Gladiator because it is a fifteen and he was fourteen at that time, and it really doesn't make sense, you will let him out for a fag break every fifty minutes and then you ring me up. ...

Whilst Mrs. Miles is conscientious in terms of her mothering duties and therefore in many ways conforms to official constructions of the good parent (see, for example, Home Office, 1998), this work is not rewarded financially. Nor is her voluntary work for the domestic violence and drug support organizations.

Martin's decision to follow what his mother calls the 'drugs route' is arguably a response to his mother's economic marginalization. For Martin, selling drugs is more economically productive than attending school.

The schools that Martin has attended and the college he currently attends are also subject to distributive injustice. These institutions do not have sufficient resources to cope with the multiple challenges they face. Martin is just one of a number of 'disruptive' students and there are other challenges apart from those posed by such students that these institutions have to deal with because of the disadvantaged socio-economic context within which they are located. This in turn means that Martin and the other young people who attend these institutions do not get access to the same quantity or quality of educational resources that are available to young people living in better off areas. For example, one possible reason why Mrs. Miles is not listened to is that the educational professionals she has to deal with simply do not have the time to listen. Like Mrs. Miles, these professionals are also stretched. This may be one of the reasons why they do not always turn up to meetings which is a source of frustration for Mrs. Miles:

> These meetings never consist of the people who are meant to be there.
> There is always a few of them missing or all of them. They are never all there.

It is also possible that the reason Mrs. Miles had to fight so hard to get her son assessed by relevant professionals was the reluctance of the local authority to make the necessary investment because of their own funding shortages.

Mrs. Miles and Martin also suffer injustices of recognition. Mrs. Miles' sense of this injustice is captured in her comment about how if she had lived in a big house, had a husband and Martin was not mixed race, then he may have got more favourable treatment. It is also captured in her story about the teacher who shamed Martin for effectively not being able to afford the right kind of shoes. She also tells other stories of misrecognition. For example, she says that because her son was constructed as a problem she considers herself to be one: 'Because I was a mother with a problem child I suppose, I always felt inadequate because I had a problem child'. And she talks movingly about how her sons' experiences of racism have had a deep-seated effect on their psyches (although she is also amazingly optimistic about the possibility of them somehow shedding the psychological effects of the racism they have experienced as children):

> Oh yes. They have got huge worth problems and valuing themselves. There have been times when they have been depressed for weeks and weeks, and then eventually you would get out of them that the kids had called them something. So yeah, they will carry that for the rest of their lives until they get to a place where [they] can think, 'hold on a minute here' and realize what other people think is not, their perception isn't reality, you know, all that stuff … Put it this way, if I had known this community was like that I wouldn't have moved here … I have had the police out and everything. In them days, they didn't do anything. Nowadays they might but in them days it was 'oh well never mind', push it under the carpet kind of thing.

The story also demonstrates how the education system can produce forms of what Young calls cultural imperialism. The narrow focus of Martin's secondary school on academic success and conventional academic measures of performance means that those young people, like Martin, who do not conform to conventional expectations of how to be a student may feel that what is valuable to them is not valued by the system.

Finally, the story illustrates forms of associational injustice. There is currently in the UK and elsewhere a high-profile official policy discourse of parental and community involvement, partnership and participation but this story suggests that Martin's secondary school (like some of those studied by Vincent, 2000) and his college were operating with a limited notion of parental involvement. Mrs. Miles was expected to be involved to the extent that she needs to be prepared to collect her son at times when the school or college can not cope; and the college is, in Mrs. Miles' words, 'good' about showing her the work he is doing and the teachers there do ask her for her opinion on how they should deal with Martin. However, more generally, Mrs. Miles' story is one of having to literally fight the system to try and get her son access to a formal education. This is partly a result of distributive injustices, some of which I have identified above. The patterns of association Mrs. Miles is subject to privilege those with the requisite forms of economic, social and cultural capital. However, having said that, it is important not to over-simplify the highly differentiated and complex nature of parents' encounters with educational institutions: even middle-class parents with the 'right' kinds of social and cultural capital, particularly those with children identified as having learning or behavioural problems, can experience the same kinds of frustrations that Mrs. Miles describes. As Vincent (2000, p. 136) puts it, middle-class parents 'do not all find schools to be inevitably "malleable"'.

## Conflicts between Dimensions of Justice

So far I have used the case of the Mileses to illustrate the multi-dimensional nature of justice. Here I want to use it to illustrate a key tension between Young's dimensions of justice, that is the tension between the demands of distributive and recognitional justice which is identified and theorized in Fraser's critical development of Young's work (Fraser, 1997). In order for resources to be justly redistributed it is necessary for certain individuals and institutions to be identified—and therefore labelled—as in need of additional resourcing. But that process of identification and labelling may result in social marginalization and personal devaluation. This is one example of what Fraser (1997) has called the redistribution-recognition dilemma. As a student with learning/behavioural difficulties, Martin belongs to an oppressed group which Fraser would categorize as bivalent. That is, he is distributively disadvantaged in terms of his access to educational resources and culturally marginalized through being labelled as a 'problem' child. Thus his inequitable situation requires distributive and recognitional remedies. The problem is that the two kinds of remedies are to some degree contradictory in so far as they work in opposite directions. Redistributive remedies involve processes of categorization. In the case of education these render students such as Martin, and indeed the kinds of schools that have a disproportionate number of children like Martin in them, as at best 'needy' and at worst 'a problem'.[5]

## The Mediated Nature of Just Practices

Let me now turn to a discussion of the mediated nature of just practices. Even if Martin's teachers are committed to more egalitarian practices—and some may well be—there will almost inevitably be other concerns that interact with those commitments to shape the actions that these teachers take. These concerns might relate to other normative commitments the teachers hold that fall outside the domain of justice. For example, some of Martin's teachers might value forms of social order that necessitate the exclusion of Martin from their classes. For such teachers there will be a conflict between their desire for social order and their desire to give Martin the same access to educational opportunities as his more compliant classmates. In resolving this conflict such teachers may well end up making choices which involve sacrificing justice for the sake of order.

But teachers' freedom of manoeuvre in relation to promoting more socially just practices might also be constrained by countervailing pressures that are not of their own making. For example, there are currently strong pressures placed on English schools by government policies of target-setting to focus on students who can perform well in tests. In turn, this, combined with insufficient resourcing, puts pressure on schools to exclude students like Martin to prevent them from disrupting the learning of others.

Therefore competing norms and external constraints mean that we cannot simply think in an abstract way about what is the most socially just thing to do. That is, we cannot directly translate principle into practice, but we need to think about what it is reasonable to expect given the competing concerns and constraints which help to shape social action in particular instances. For instance, in Martin's case, because of resource and policy pressures, there is little scope for Martin's teachers to allow him to participate in decisions about his own learning (i.e. there is little scope for what might be viewed as relatively advanced forms of associational justice). Therefore, in this particular context, the teachers letting him out for a cigarette break every fifty minutes might be viewed as a social justice success.

## The Level- and Context-dependency of Just Practices

It is also important to bear in mind that different practices are appropriate and possible at different levels and in different contexts of action. To illustrate my point about level-dependency, let me briefly compare the possibilities of action for three kinds of agents who are differently positioned vis-à-vis the education system—policy makers, trade unions and teachers.

Policy makers have scope to make resource decisions (e.g. in the case of the UK, reallocating money spent on the war in Iraq to schools) which could help the professionals working with Martin to give Martin more of the kind of attention he needs or which would give the professionals more time to relate in more respectful ways with Martin and his mother.

Trade unions, on the other hand, are not in a position to redistribute resources in this way but they can try to put pressure on the government to shift priorities through campaigning, industrial action etc. In England, for instance, the National Union of Teachers has organized campaigns against the national tests (SATs) which many believe are distorting the curriculum with unjust consequences.

Finally, Martin's teachers also do not have much power over resource distribution, but they can choose to engage in collective action for social justice ends, like boycotting SATs. They can also take a position, as individuals, that they will endeavour as far as possible, given the pressures they are under, to treat Martin and his mother in respectful ways. So the point I am making here is that what counts as a successful just practice is likely to differ according to the level of enactment.

What counts as a successful just practice might also differ according to the context. For example, another student exhibiting the forms of behaviour that Martin's mother is concerned about but who lives in a more affluent community with better resourced schools and with teachers under less strain may find himself better integrated in the school and more valued and respected by his teachers. That is to say teachers in this scenario would have more time and mental space to engage in the kinds of just practices that would be a struggle for teachers in Martin's school.[6]

## Conclusion

In this paper I have not proposed a particular set of criteria for judging justice. Nor have I proposed a set of policies for achieving justice. Rather what I have begun to do in arguing for a contextualized approach to understanding justice is to sketch out a method—or analytical lens—for helping us to read and evaluate claims about justice in education. This method involves:

a) looking at the multi-dimensional nature of justice;
b) looking at the tensions between different dimensions of justice;
c) being sensitive to the mediated nature of just practices; and
d) being sensitive to differences in the contexts and levels within which justice is enacted.

This focus upon the contextualized nature of just practices, whilst not explicitly set out in these terms in Young's work, is, I would suggest, a logical consequence of taking seriously Young's concern with processes and procedures of justice at all levels of social interaction.

The attention to the specificity of local contexts should also remind us that judgements about what counts as justice in education can not be divorced from judgements about what is possible. Because in the real world principles do not translate precisely into practice, just practices can only ever meet with partial degrees of success. So in evaluating justice practices, judgements about what counts as success need to be made in the light of considerations about the particular justice conflicts, the mediation of justice, and the contexts and levels of enactment which impinge on the practices being evaluated.

Although in the example I have used I talked about the social justice implications of working in different local contexts within one particular national system—the English system—it is also important to think about the issues I have discussed here in relation to the task of comparing national education systems. In particular, we need to consider the extent and ways in which different histories, social and cultural configurations and different sets of constraints mean that different justice dimensions are relatively fore-grounded—or alternatively neglected—within different national contexts. We also need to consider how these different histories, configurations and constraints contribute to contrasting patterns of success.

On the other hand, there is a danger of moving from a position which takes differences in the contexts of enactment seriously to an extreme form of relativism which rejects the possibility or desirability of any fixed normative positions. I would want to strongly resist these kinds of slippage. In any system there will be people—like Martin—who face multiple forms of oppression and who are marginalized in various ways. I would suggest that any model of justice must face the challenge of reducing the inequities of distribution, recognition and association which oppress and marginalize groups represented by people such as Martin. It is imperative that debates about the contestability and context dependency of justice are used to contribute to the development of more just practices in education and not to detract from the moral and political obligation to promote justice.

## Notes

1. This paper grows out of joint work I am engaged in with Alan Cribb which seeks to marry ethical and sociological analysis to produce a more ethically reflexive sociology of education.
2. The initiative was called the Education Action Zones initiative. The title of the project was 'Education Action Zones: paving a third way?' It was funded by the UK Economic and Social Research Council (award no. R000238046). In this paper I am using fictional names for people, institutions and places to protect the anonymity of 'Martin' and his mother, 'Mrs. Miles', and others who were involved or referred to in the research. I am grateful to Marie Lall who carried out the interview with Mrs. Miles and to the other research team members Marny Dickson, David Halpin, Sally Power and Geoff Whitty for giving me permission to use this interview here.
3. For the purposes of this paper, I am taking what Mrs. Miles says at face value. It may be that others involved in the events she describes would contest her version of these events and may want to argue, for example, that the Mileses have not been subject to the range of unjust practices that I am identifying here. However, since I am simply using the story to draw attention to the different kinds of in/justice that can exist, the accuracy of the story is not relevant here.
4. The distributive conception of social justice might be constructed in such a way that it also encompasses what I am delineating here as the other dimensions of justice. My concern here is less with the labels than with the different dimensions that the labels denote.
5. Fraser does advocate a form of remedy that she argues 'finesses' the dilemma. Rather than 'affirmative' strategies which seek to affirm the rights of oppressed groups to be treated equally, she advocates 'transformative' strategies which involve deconstructing existing social categories and radically reconstructing relations of production. However, I would want to question how far it is possible to eliminate all hierarchical forms of social categorization and thus I think we need to question analyses which trade on this possibility.
6. For empirical accounts of the different possibilities available to teachers working in different socio-economic contexts, see Gewirtz (1998) and Thrupp (1998).

## References

Cribb, A. & Gewirtz, S. (2003) Towards a Sociology of Just Practices: an analysis of plural conceptions of justice, in: C. Vincent (ed.), *Social Justice, Education and Identity* (London, Routledge).

Fraser, N. (1997) *Justice Interruptus* (New York, Routledge).

Gewirtz, S. (1998) Can All Schools be Successful? An exploration of the determinants of school 'success', *Oxford Review of Education*, 24:4, pp. 439–457.

Home Office (1998) *Supporting Families: A Consultation Document*, Cm 3991 (London, The Stationery Office).

Land, H. (1999) New Labour, New Families, in: H. Dean & R. Woods (eds) *Social Policy Review*, 11, pp. 127–44 (Luton, Social Policy Association).

Power, S. & Gewirtz, S. (2001) Reading Education Action Zones, *Journal of Education Policy*, 16:1, pp. 38–51.

Rawls, J. (1972) *A Theory of Justice* (Oxford, Clarendon Press).

Taylor, C. (1994) *Multiculturalism* (Princeton, NJ, Princeton University Press).

Thrupp, M. (1998) The Art of the Possible. organising and managing high and low socio-economic schools, *Journal of Education Policy*, 13:2 pp. 197–219.

Vincent, C. (2000) *Including Parents? Education, Citizenship and Parental Agency* (Buckingham, Open University Press).

Young, I. M. (1990) *Justice and the Politics of Difference* (Princeton, NJ, Princeton University Press).

# 6

# Iris Marion Young's Imaginations of Gift Giving: Some implications for the teacher and the student

SIMONE GALEA
*University of Malta*

Iris Marion Young considers differences and communication in a democracy as mutually constitutive. Differences nourish deliberations, which in usual democratic situations are aimed towards consensus (Young, 1997b). However Young's politics of difference also sees communication itself as a source of transformation, of the creation of differences.

Within such a democratic scenario, Iris Marion Young develops the notion of asymmetric reciprocity (Young, 1997a). The communicative ethics underlying such a notion rethinks the maxim that is taken for granted, that a person has to put herself in place of another to really understand that other. This maxim is usually thought of as a reliable way to ensure that one's actions *vis-à-vis* another take account of the standpoint of the other.

Iris Marion Young argues that such ethical guidelines are a real obstacle to good communication between people, as their differences are obscured by obligations to imagine their selves as being the same as that of others. There is always an asymmetry between one and the other which cannot be overcome by simply imagining her thoughts, feelings and intentions. Young describes these relationships as being similar to relationships of gift giving.

In fact, her notion of asymmetric reciprocity is developed along Derrida's ideas about the gift (Derrida, 1992). Usually we think of gift giving as something two persons give and receive from each other. However, according to Derrida gift giving cannot be understood as a circular exchange of things. For one can say that she has given something when she expects nothing in return and one can say she has received something when she has given nothing back. It is this ideal condition of asymmetry that makes the gift possible.

Iris Marion Young has taken up this notion of asymmetry of the gift to argue that when one imagines oneself in another's position, all one sees is a mirror image of oneself. This putting oneself in place of another has been the cause of injustice to people whose places have been inhabited by others.

Young explains that the notions of gift giving and asymmetric reciprocity are ideals that have been formulated 'out of the possibilities of our interaction and our sense of lack in those interactions' (Young/Dhanda, 1999, p. 11). They raise questions about taken for granted experiences in specific contexts. However the problems within specific contexts can be manifested in other local contexts. According to Young, the ideas and thoughts generated within specific contexts can be identified as local theories. She continues to explain that theorising within a disciplinary context can be relevant to other disciplinary contexts and locations.

In this paper I shall be following Young's Foucaultian understanding of local theory. I shall take up her notions of asymmetric reciprocity and gift giving to raise some questions within the educational context of the classroom and the ethical relationships between the teacher and the student. Can teaching be considered as a gift? What are the implications of considering teaching as a form of gift giving? How do the asymmetrical relations between the teacher and the student contribute to the gift of teaching and what kinds of gifts can be given in the classroom?

The first section of the paper gives an account of some theoretical debates that gave rise to Young's notion of asymmetric reciprocity. I shall then explain the notion in relation to the idea of gift giving and talk about its relevance to learning situations. The next section will deal with the main question of the paper namely the implications of envisaging teaching as gift giving. Taking note of the problems discussed in the previous section I shall talk about the ideal imaginations of gift giving to suggest pedagogies that are based on Iris Marion Young's communicative ethics.

## Putting Our Selves in Dialogue

Iris Marion Young presents her idea that relations are asymmetrical in reaction to Seyla Benhabib's revisiting of Habermas' theory of communication (Young, 1997a). Benhabib envisages communication situations as perfectly symmetrical and believes that persons engaged in dialogue can adopt the positions and perspectives of other persons. Young states that such a theory of communicative ethics is too unifying and that the concept of reversibility of standpoints can annihilate differences for the sake of consensual agreement.

She argues that asymmetrical reciprocal relations are more just because they morally respect the particular differences of persons involved in communicative relations. One takes account of the other in conversation but this reciprocity must not ignore the different historical, social and cultural positions of the other. Reciprocal relations do not necessitate precise overlaps between people. Reciprocity entails moral respect in that one acknowledges the differences between oneself and the other and listens to her in a continuous attempt towards further understanding. Listening, acknowledging and understanding the other are quite different from putting oneself in the position of another; imagining what one would feel and/or think in another's place, and attributing these thoughts and feelings to the other. Putting oneself in place of another brings about many misconceptions, misunderstandings and injustices. One can imagine oneself in a disabled body. One can think and publicly state that such a life is not worth living. Such declarations not only muffle the voices of disabled people but are used to render people more disabled by encouraging others to deny them services (Young, 1997a, pp. 41–42). I can live a day in the life of somebody and this can stimulate my imaginative response to how she feels, lives and acts but I can never say that I have understood how she feels until I listen to her. Differentiating myself from her will help me realise all the more that there is considerable distance between us, which can be breached by speaking and listening.

One has to be careful about ways of speaking and listening. I may have listened to somebody today and understood her experience and her position in relation to myself and to others. However I cannot say that I have fully understood that person. Persons can change their positions because of new experiences. They can give different meanings to those experiences due to relations with others that have contributed to their re-positioning. Therefore communicative efforts to understand each other are always in transition because communication itself changes who we are. In this respect, communication acts are acts of teaching and learning. I can be taught by others that my perspectives are partial. I can learn that I am trying to solve problems which others are trying to solve and learn that their approach and perspectives are different. Young explains that:

> Communication is a creative enterprise that presupposes an irreplaceability of each person's perspective so that each learns something new, beyond herself or himself, from interaction with others (Young, 1997a, p. 51).

## Asymmetries of Teaching and Learning

Iris Marion Young makes a crucial point here. Learning and teaching necessitate an asymmetry between people. This is what we take for granted in thinking of relationships between teachers and pupils. The act of teaching is seen as founded on inequalities of experiences and knowledge between the teacher and the student. The teacher gives something which she has and which she is, which the student does not have. In this respect many teachers think of teaching as a vocation; giving without taking back; giving without expecting anything in return. Thought of in this way, teaching goes along with the asymmetrical ideal of gift giving presented by Derrida.

> If there is gift, the given of the gift (that which one gives, that which is given, the gift as given thing or as act of donation) must not come back to the giving (let us not already say to the subject, to the donor). It must not circulate, it must not be exchanged, it must not in any case be exhausted, as a gift, by the process of exchange, by the movement of circulation of the circle in the form of return to the point of departure (Derrida, 1992, p. 7).

> For there to be a gift, it is necessary that the donee not give back, amortize, reimburse, acquit himself, enter into a contract and that he never have contracted a debt (Derrida, 1992, p. 3).

Upon reflection, one recognises that a teaching situation does not exactly satisfy these conditions. Derrida himself refers to relationships of teaching and learning to point to their symmetries of giving and taking. For someone to give a lesson another person has to give attention to the lesson. The teacher expects something back: attention.

> (T)his is an unsigned but effective contract between us, indispensable to what is happening here, namely that you accord, lend, or give some attention and some meaning to what I myself am doing, for example by giving a lecture (Derrida, 1992, p. 11).

Considering teaching within the ideal asymmetric conditions of gift giving described by Derrida has other important implications for a philosophy of teaching. The gift giving structure of giving and not being given anything back, can imply that relations between teachers and students are monological and that there is a unidirectional transmission of knowledge from the teacher to the student. Thinking of the teacher as the giver constructs the student as a passive receiver whose function as a listener and interpreter is trivialised. Nevertheless, within the sender-receiver model the teacher is already given something back—importance and privilege (Garrison & Kimball, 1993). Garrison and Kimball argue that within this conduit model the teacher as a giver is given priority: what, to whom and how it is given are trivialised.

Proponents of dialogical education would clearly find this incompatible with their philosophy of democratic education. Democracy, as Dewey suggests, is a way of life that is to be encouraged within the classroom. Lessons are developed through co-operation between the teacher and the student—a mutual sharing and creation of their knowledge rather than a one way transmission of existing and established knowledge.

Dewey's philosophy represents the teacher and the student standing together facing a problem. Robert Young (1992) explains that there is yet another representation of this relationship (based on Habermas' communicative ethics): the teacher and the student facing each other in resolving the problem. This positioning of persons looking at each other may be a more accurate representation of persons in positions of gift giving.

Nevertheless Dewey's and Habermas' images both represent consensual co-ordination between the teacher and the student, that do not completely break the circle of exchange as Derrida would have it. On the other hand the giving-receiving model would necessitate unequal relations that are unacceptable to teachers whose democratic philosophies envisage students as active participating persons in social conditions of equity and equality.

One has to remember, however, that a democratic understanding of the relationship between the teacher and the student draws on the asymmetries of the relationship. Asymmetry is brought about by the very fact that the teacher exercises her professional privilege and a specialised knowledge base to bring about democratic learning environments in schools and classrooms. Democratic education is as paradoxical as the asymmetry of the gift. The gift is considered to be a gift when it is not recognised as a gift. Democratic education is possible when teachers 'in the very promotion of social reconstruction towards democracy they have to engage in certain non-democratic practices' (Harris, 1994, p. 68).

## Delivering Gifts

Thinking of teaching as a gift challenges the usual meanings we give to teaching and more deeply the principles and values that ground our teachings. The main challenge is to think of teaching as an asymmetrical relation between student and teacher, yet at the same be vigilant to the kind of asymmetry that is allowed within the relationship. At the same time, as Young explains, one has to take note of the contexts within which asymmetrical relationships take shape.

Nigel Blake, Paul Smeyers, Richard Smith and Paul Standish (1998) argue that teaching cannot be considered as an act of gift giving where education takes place within an economy of exchange.

> Let us see this economy of exchange. The efforts of the teacher and pupil are directed by these outcomes. What is to be learned is made clear to the students while these processes must in turn be transparent and available to scrutiny. The teacher becomes a learning resource. This economy of exchange is suggested also in the vocabulary of 'stakeholders' learning entitlements, vouchers and contracts. Efficiency and effectiveness become eminently rational criteria in this smooth running system of circulation (Blake *et al.*, 1998, p. 81).

Blake, Smeyers, Smith and Standish explain that such processes have many things in common with controlled and highly efficient systems of delivery.

The impersonality of the act of delivery questions our taken-for-granted idiom— lesson delivery. Within this context, delivering the gift is different from giving a gift. If I am just delivering the gift the nature of the content of the gift does not really interest me. I might get a glimpse of the reactions of the one getting the gift but I wouldn't really care about the feelings, the sense of surprise and wonder that my delivery of the gift has brought about. My concern is that the gift has safely arrived at its destination. When I am asked to deliver knowledge I am concerned with visible outcomes—that I have delivered that knowledge, that it has been deposited safely within children's minds. I am not concerned about what use they make of that knowledge or the meanings and interpretations of that knowledge. What counts is that I have delivered, banked and deposited established knowledge.

These systems of delivery tend to subjugate the knowledges and experiences of students whose cultural backgrounds are different from those of the school, and to segregate them according to the degrees of compliance to school cultures. Maxine Greene (1995) believes that these systems reflect what happens and what is suggested by social and economic systems. She explains that the exchanges between the school and socio-economic order function to channel, constrain and prescribe rather than to emancipate and open up opportunities for people to create their own selves. Giving an education entails breaking up this circle of exchange.

The language of delivery has to do with what many educational theorists have described as the reproductive aspect of educational systems and educational theories themselves (Bourdieu & Passeron, 1977; Apple, 1993; Ellsworth, 1989). Delivery and reproduction may have maternal connotations, but as Irigaray explains the maternal within a phallocratic economy is understood through a language of sameness rather than being associated with processes of creation.

Teaching is often involved in the reproduction of persons. Sometimes even pedagogies that claim to be student-centred engage in reproductive acts. Student-centred approaches are said to focus around the student just as gift giving should focus on whom it is given: I can really think about the qualities and characteristics of the person and make the gift particular and individual. Nevertheless the gift is mine and at times I lapse into perceiving other people enjoying the things that I like. I see them do the thing I do and become a bit like me.

With all good intentions we do see our students becoming like us, a mirror image of ourselves. I imagine them in my place and project my own fantasies on to them.

## Making the First Move

In the previous section I explained that the main problem in considering teaching as gift giving is that it takes place within circles of exchange. The teacher gives a lesson, the student gives back the same content, social and cultural contexts give opportunities for teaching and learning but conservative returns are expected. Thinking of teaching as gift giving, however hints at the possibilities of breaking these circles of exchange. Iris Marion Young states that 'the ideal of gift giving (even though it is always imperfectly realised and sometimes more perfectly realised than others) is one where there has to be a first move, which is a moment of courage, graciousness and generosity' (Young/Dhanda, 1999, p. 11). Teaching has to have the same moment of courage in making the first move to give something, the graciousness to give something different and the generosity to give something precious.

The problem with considering teaching as a gift is that teaching acts always get some form of compensation: the act of teaching expects something back. Teaching then steps into the circle of reciprocal exchange, which Derrida sees as the destruction of the gift. On the other hand teaching becomes problematic, it is not teaching at all when reciprocity is not involved in the equation.

Young's interpretation of Derrida's notion of gift giving gives back the reciprocal dimension to the act of gift giving. Her interpretation makes it possible to view teaching as gift giving because she highlights the reciprocity that makes the gift socially and culturally meaningful. At the same time it stresses the importance of an asymmetrical relationship in acts of gift giving.

Young argues that it is not the responding moments of the relations in acts of gift giving (or teaching) that are problematic. If I am given a gift and after some time I feel like reciprocating, I cannot say that I have not been given a gift or that the gift that I shall be giving is not a gift. Gifts become questionable when they are of the same nature or involve the exchange of the same thing. As Young explains, gifts are considered to be gifts when they are qualitatively different.

This brings to mind the problems of a reproduction of knowledge, culture, socio-economic orders and the reproduction of people. Teachers should expect to be given something different from that which they have given. Students' responses that are exactly similar to what the teacher has delivered cannot be considered to be gifts that nourish the relationship between the teacher and the student. Young gives the example of having someone saying back the same thing that the other person has told her. To be given different gifts, teachers need to go beyond the usual acts of delivering.

## Ways of Giving

Teachers have to be more like specific intellectuals (Foucault, 1989). These do not speak for others because they have given others opportunities to speak for themselves. It is unrealistic to expect teachers to always act as specific intellectuals. They are expected to have the authority to say what has to be done, to say what others do not know, to give advice. However specific teachers as I may call them, know that what they say need not be totalising, conscious that suggestions to their students are made from their positions as teachers and any questions they ask receive answers specific to the particularities of their students.

It is not enough to have the teacher and the student looking at each other if they are not attentive to the different ways they speak. They also need to look at problems through their different ways. Teachers are like specific intellectuals when they understand how these differences may have been marginalised and how these differences might break circles of power and conservative exchanges. As explained at the very beginning of this paper, the basic condition for such communicative acts is an acknowledgement of the difference of the other. The teacher can face her students but she can never put herself in their place. The teacher can look at her students but she has to listen to their stories.

> A condition of our communication is that we acknowledge the difference, interval, that others drag behind them shadows and histories, scars and traces, that do not become present in our communication. Thus we must be open to learning about the other person's perspective, since we cannot take the other person's standpoint and imagine that perspective as our own (Young, 1997a, p. 53).

Earlier on I commented about the injustices of inhabiting spaces which are not our own and occupying worlds of others. However learning about these places and worlds is important. Morwenna Griffiths' (1997) metaphor of travelling opens up our imagination as to how spaces can be glimpsed, but not inhabited; how perspectives and ideas can be interpreted but not completely grasped. We can travel in different ways. Iris Marion Young (1997a) speaks about a sense of wonder that instigates serious listening to the other and a desire to question.

These ways of travelling are both relevant to the teacher and the student. Wonder is the 'openness to the newness and mystery of the other person' (Young, 1997a, p. 56). The student wonders what lesson the teacher will give today or she may wonder if she knows the solution to that problem. This sense of wonder at not knowing is what instigates listening to the teacher. The teacher develops her lessons through a sense of wonder, an expectancy of how her lesson will be accepted. Lessons are developed after wondering what the needs and interests of the student are. Again the teacher has to listen to travel towards her students.

Questions are also ways of showing our openness to learning about the other. Questioning also invokes a sense of wonder. Young remarks that there is a thin line that can easily be crossed between a sense of wonder that shows respect to the other and one which intends to oppress and dominate.

The same applies to questioning and in particular questioning techniques used by the teacher. Robert Young (1992) states that questioning is a favourite teaching technique. However one must reflect 'When a question is not a question?' (Young, 1992, p. 90). There are more productive questions, where the teacher asks questions to motivate students to reach conclusions or ask questions themselves, or question what the teacher is saying. Then there are questions that are intended for students to give back what has been given. There are questions that satisfy the teacher's curiosity. Students become exotic learning objects for manipulation. Certain investigative modes are frequently accepted as ways by which teachers devise their coping strategies.

Student profiles are also a professionally accepted practice that satisfy the teacher's sense of wonder. They initiate a process of understanding students. However profiles are gifts from other lands, souvenirs of experiences of travelling that instigate us to travel further to get to know other subjugated histories. In similar ways, pupils profiles are only an invitation to a deeper communication between he teacher and the student; the desire of the teacher to get to know what the student has to say about herself and to give the time to listen to her stories.

## Conclusion

In thinking about teaching as a gift I have mentioned practices of teaching that involve asymmetrical relations between teachers and students. I have spoken about the contexts within which gifts and lessons are given and how these need to be changed for reproductive circles of exchange to be broken. It involves a sense of not knowing the other completely but knowing the power networks inside educational institutions as well as the powers of speaking, speaking for and not speaking.

Gifts are possible when teaching is particularly inclined to surprise the person who is getting the gift and to make the giver wonder about the other's responses. I intend to give a gift just as the planned lesson but the lesson cannot be completely controlled. The way it has been received might give some appreciation or disappointment but what the student has done with the gift can only be imagined by the teacher.

In this paper I have suggested ways in which gifts of teaching can be something special; an opening to newness. In considering teaching as a gift one has to acknowledge that the best gifts of teaching are those moments of not giving. When the teacher gives nothing, she can give her students and herself time to think about their interactions and the space to make themselves differently in the light of their interactions. These moments of not giving give time and space for teachers and students to become different from each other and from what they have been. Moments of not giving will still be involved in relations of reciprocity. However it is a kind of reciprocity where differences and transformations take shape. Teaching and learning are moments of giving and not giving. They can be breeding grounds for asymmetries that ensure creative communicative exchanges.

## References

Apple, M. (1982) *The Politics of Official Knowledge* (New York, Routledge).

Blake, N., Smeyers, P., Smith R. & Standish P. (1998) Giving Someone a Lesson, in: *Thinking Again: Education After Postmodernism* (London, Bergin & Garvey).

Bourdieu, P. & Passeron, J. C. (1977) *Reproduction in Education, Society and Culture* (London, Sage).

Derrida, J. (1992) *Given Time: Counterfeit Money* (Chicago, University of Chicago Press).

Ellsworth, E. (1989) Why Doesn't This Feel Empowering? Working through repressive myths of critical pedagogy, *Harvard Educational Review*, 59.

Foucault, M. (1989) The End of the Monarchy of Sex, in: *Foucault Live* (USA, Semiotext(e)).

Garrison, J. & Kimball, S. (1993) Dialoguing Across Differences: Three hidden barriers, http://www.ed.uiuc.edu/COE/EPS (Yearbook/93-docs).

Greene, M. (1995) *Releasing the Imagination* (California, Jossey-Bass Publishers).

Griffiths, M. (1997) Why Teachers and Philosophers Need Each Other: Philosophy and educational research, *Cambridge Journal of Education*, 27:2.

Harris, K. (1993) *Teachers: Constructing the Future* (London, The Falmer Press).

Young, I. M. & Dhanda, M. (1999) Interview with Iris Marion Young. *Women's Philosophy Review 1999*.

Young, I. M. (1997a) Asymmetrical Reciprocity: On moral respect, wonder and enlarged thought, in: *Intersecting Voices Dilemmas of Gender, Political Philosophy and Policy* (Princeton, NJ, Princeton University Press).

Young, I. M. (1997b) Communication and the Other: Beyond deliberative democracy, in: *Intersecting Voices: Dilemmas of Gender, Political Philosophy and Policy* (Princeton, NJ, Princeton University Press).

Young, R. (1992) *Critical Theory and Classroom Talk* (Clevedon, Multilingual Matters Ltd.).

# 7

# Education in the Context of Structural Injustice: A symposium response

IRIS MARION YOUNG
*University of Chicago*

## I. Distributive Justice in Education

Several of the authors in this symposium, including Eisenberg and Enslin, note that I have argued that dominant paradigms of justice focus too narrowly on issues of distribution. Theorists working within that paradigm do not sufficiently recognize how social structures raise additional issues of justice, such as those concerning decision making power, division of labor, being disadvantaged by dominant norms, and freedom of culture expression (Young, 2000a, chapter 1).[1] As Eisenberg emphasizes, this criticism of focus on distributive issues does not imply a rejection of concern for distributive justice. I'll begin, then, by reminding us of the huge issues of distributive justice facing education in most societies today.

Policy makers and corporate leaders still pay lip service to the idea that education is the wrench that will close the inequality gap in societies of class privilege. In the middle decades of the twentieth century in the United States, the form and extent of public investment in education lent some backing to this promise. Free public quality education still receives strong financial support in many European countries, though recent decades of immigration have tended to produce segregated groups whose youth are alienated from and poorly resourced by the education systems. Some Asian countries, such as Japan and Korea, fund education at a high level fairly equitably.

In most of the world, however, it remains true that the amount and quality of education a child receives is largely determined by his or her parents' level of wealth and income. While this class reproduction of educational privilege has always been true in the United States, in the last two decades the fact has expanded to Dickensian proportions. The consensus has become that providing children with a quality education is the responsibility of parents primarily, not communities. Every year more ballot initiatives or legislative bills calling for increased public funding for education are defeated, even as schools crumble and class sizes increase, and more subjects fall off the curriculum. What kind of arguments will persuade Americans that cross-class investment in education is a good reason to raise taxes?

The situation is far worse, of course, in most of the rest of the world. Most countries in Latin America, Asian and Africa charge fees for schooling. In many these fees have risen because of structural adjustment programs, even as the same programs make families poorer. Many poor families cannot afford to send their children to school not only because of the fees, but because they need these children to work in order for the families to survive. Penny Enslin is quite right to raise the issue of transnational justice in education. Before we talk about 'intervening' in the sovereign affairs of countries to force or demand that they educate for democracy, however, it would be appropriate to pressure the rich countries of the world into transferring resources to enable basic education everywhere. Canceling the debts that force many developing countries to implement structural adjustment programs would be an easy and good beginning. Debt cancellation does not even require a transfer of resources; as in the Jubilee philosophy, it simply means that all parties start over with what they presently have.

It would be absurd to assert that a politics of difference plays no role in the underfunding of education. Gender difference intersects with the distribution of education opportunity everywhere. Where education is relatively costly, and girls are socialized primarily for duties in the home, it seems rational to many to spend scarce resources first on the education of boys and men. A revolutionary change in the extent of educational opportunity for girls and women is one of the major achievements of the second half of the twentieth century in more well to do parts of the world. Penny Enslin calls for 'intervention' by these more well off countries to effect more education for girls in those places where sexism rules more boldly. She does not say precisely what she means by intervention. Recent military adventures ought to demonstrate the imprudence of trying to change social norms by force, never mind the justice of doing so.

Frazer and Eisenberg both emphasize that I have conceptualized domination and oppression as the wider categories that name injustice. While unfair distribution of goods and resources are often part of these injustices, they have additional forms and supports. Three of the most important of these are the social division of labor, normalization, and decision making power. Each of the next three sections situates some of the essays in this symposium in terms of these issues of justice, and tries to clarify my position on them.

## II. Hierarchical Division of Labor

Modern industrial societies everywhere today assume a division between professional and managerial work, on the one hand, and service, manufacturing, and clerical labor, on the other. In most of these societies, occupying a professional position is what Michael Walzer calls a 'dominant' good (Walzer, 1983). Professional occupations tend to bring with them many of the goods society has to offer: income, job stability, high status, workplace autonomy, often significant decision making power, opportunities for recognition, and opportunities for developing and using expertise or creativity. The basic structure of this division of labor is, moreover, hierarchical: the most desirable positions are relatively scarce; they also are positions in which those in them expect obedience and/or deference from those in lower status positions, and usually receive it.

In advanced industrial societies most people appear not to consider this structure unjust, even though it entails inequalities of all kinds—wealth, recognition, and power. Most people consider this structure to be the way things are. The structure is usually justified on two grounds: it is the most efficient way to organize an economy, and it is fair because the system offers equal opportunity for everyone to compete for the best positions. As in a game, it is legitimate for most people to be losers and only a few to be winners, because everyone has had a chance to compete.

In an economy that produces a large number of goods, I believe that a structure of this sort, which condemns most people to positions requiring little skill, few opportunities to develop and exercise capacities, positions which lack autonomy and must often be subservient to others, is unjust. I will not take the space here fully to argue for this judgment. Doing so involves appeal both to equality of respect and a right to develop capabilities. What I wish to do here is remind us of the complicity of educational processes in reproducing and legitimating this hierarchical division of labor.

Avigail Eisenberg refers to the relationship between the educational system and the doctrines of equal opportunity and merit that legitimate hierarchy in liberal democratic societies. Both I and others have argued that the standards according to which performance is evaluated in educational institutions and on the standardized tests they increasingly use, often operate in biased ways to pass the privilege of middle-class white Anglo male parents on to their sons. I will elaborate on this dynamic of normalization in the next section.

The case of Mrs. Miles and her son, detailed in Sharon Gewirtz's paper, is a poignant reminder that the educational system of most advanced industrial societies functions as much to produce losers as winners. On the whole, educational systems are not forgiving and supportive enough of students who for one reason or another do not easily fit into the disciplines and routines that mimic the professional life those who succeed are destined for—children with physical or mental disabilities, poor children, children whose parents are unable to monitor and help with homework, children who poorly know the language of instruction, children who face racist or ethnocentric prejudice from teachers, other children and neighbors. According to chilly classroom climate studies, girl children continue to be relatively invisible to their teachers, at the same time that they continue to be liable to sexual harassment and gender prejudice. To the extent that teachers, curricula, and school administrative policy do not actively seek to counter these tendencies for social difference to become learning disadvantage, they help create lifetime losers by labeling these children failures.

Because there are few opportunities in advanced industrial societies for adults who decide that they would like to try again to obtain good pre-college credentials by studying full time, those who fail to get them when they were young are usually condemned to the lower ranks of the occupational hierarchy for the rest of their lives. The main injustice of this system, I think, is the structure of the division of labor in which most positions lack autonomy, significant remuneration, status, and opportunities to learn more skills. To the extent that education systems encourage people to accept that structure as necessary and allow most people to wind up as losers, they contribute to this structural injustice.

## III. Normalization

With the term 'normalization' I refer to processes that construct experience and capacities of some social segments into standards against which all are measured and some found wanting, or deviant. Ronald Beiner appears to find the idea that normalization raises issues of justice puzzling, so I am glad for the opportunity to make myself clearer. While not identical to issues of a hierarchical division of labor, the two interact in important ways in the occupation and educational system.

The primary form of 'difference' with which my work has always been concerned is that which appears as structural inequality. Frazer especially draws attention to the aspect of my theorizing that attends to how we dwell in social structures in which we are positioned in relation to one another in ways that tend to privilege some of us in some respects and disadvantage others. Unfair normalization occurs when institutions and practices expect individuals to exhibit certain kinds of attributes and/or behaviors that are assumed as the norm, but which some individuals are unable to exhibit, or can only exhibit at an unfair cost to themselves, because they are different.

Let me illustrate this first with the situation of people with disabilities. Only recently in the United States and some other countries has the stigma and marginalization which is the lot of many people with disabilities begun to be understood as an injustice. In many other parts of the world it remains simply a natural fact that some people are physically or mentally deviant, and on this account cannot lay claim to equal respect and equal opportunity. Even in societies that have recognized formal equality for people with disabilities, however, most suffer from the harms of normalization.

Here is what I mean. Buildings, public events, workplace arrangements and rules, tend to assume that their users and inhabitants are all sighted and hearing walkers with strength and dexterity enough to open heavy doors and stamina enough to work steadily or sit still for hours without a rest period. People with those attributes set the standard for what can be expected of everyone. To the extent that many people do not meet this standard in one way or another, the structure construes this as a problem with *them*, rather than with how the system has made the buildings or how it designs equipment, or what its rules are. The people with disabilities are then usually excluded from the activities or opportunities these institutions offer to those who fall within the norms. When the institutions make an effort to accommodate people with disabilities, it is usually grudgingly, and in a way that continues to call attention to their deviance and not afford them equality opportunity and respect (see Young, 2000b).

Most people, and most theorists of justice, continue to construct people with disabilities as 'outliers,' not falling within the parameters of primary issues of justice.[2] When we gather all the people who do not fit the above standard into a group, however, as are talking about a large proportion of any given population. A few philosophers have ventured the following radical proposal, however, which I endorse: the justice of a society ought to be judged according to how well it can respond to the needs of everyone, whatever their physical or mental capacities, without stigma or humiliation, and without they or their care givers sacrificing opportunities for developing skills and participating meaningfully in social and economic life.[3]

This is a tall order, to be sure, but we should not trim our ideals of justice just because we find the task of measuring up to them too large. While I am not an expert, I have the impression that there have been major changes in philosophies of education and pedagogy in the last century regarding people with disabilities. Educators believe, and have data to support, that nearly everyone is educable, that having physical or mental impairments need not block the ability to develop sophisticated verbal, technical and social skills which institutions can productively employ and which other people can enjoy. There remains much to be done to reform the attitudes and abilities of educators and educational institutions to enable people with disabilities both to develop their capacities and be include din activities and institutions with others on bases of equality and respect. The wider society, however, has not even caught up with fields of education in affording people with disabilities economic and occupational opportunity, access to leisure activities on a par with others, and visibility in public life.

Taking this set of cases as paradigmatic, this is what one major interpretation of a politics of difference means: that no one should be stigmatized in status or disadvantaged in their access to the resources necessary for a basic standard of well being because their physical or mental abilities differ from a majority, or because of socio-cultural attributes into which they have been socialized by a community. Processes of normalization produce such stigmatization and disadvantage. They elevate the experience and capacities of some social segments into standards against which all people are measured. In this process attributes, comportments, or ways of life that are 'normal' in the sense of exhibited by a majority or by dominant social segments come also to have the connotation of being best. To the extent that other people do not fit or fail to measure up to these standards because of their bodily capacities, group-specific socialized habits and comportments, or culture membership or way of life, they tend to be stigmatized and disadvantaged in their access to benefits. The norms that function to stigmatize or disadvantage are usually embedded in the assumptions under which institutions operate, and often the people who make decisions in them are not aware of the assumptions or their consequences.

Does a critique of normalization processes as often producing injustice imply a rejection of norms as such, either ethical norms, or institutional rules and expectation of behavior and achievement? I don't think so. Some norms are morally legitimate. What are the criteria for determining which are? Norms are morally acceptable when their purpose is to promote equal respect or to facilitate inclusive social cooperation, or when they further the particular mission of institutions and organizations without entailing disrespect, or systematic disadvantage for some groups of people.

Much, though not all, of what we call sexism is a consequence of processes of normalization, especially as manifest in institutions such as schools and many workplaces when explicit exclusion and discrimination are no longer common. These institutions tend to assume the normal body as a male body. Women who are present in them are not supposed to call attention to the specific bodily differences that derive from their reproductive biology, but which often must affect their interaction with these institutions. Thus women who are menstruating, pregnant, or lactating are under pressure to keep these facts as secret as possible and cannot expect that the institutions in which they wish to earn respect for their achievements and productivity will accommodate their differentiated needs for private space, breaks, special equipment, and so on.[4]

Masculinist normalization isn't only about a mismatch between norms and bodies, however. A quarter century of feminist theory and empirical research has uncovered myriad ways that public institutions of earning, achievement and honor tend to assume a masculine life style and typically masculine forms of comportment as normative; thus they often disadvantage the many women and some men who deviate from them. Fast track professional jobs either assume their occupants have no children or that someone else cares for them; deals get done on the golf course or in the poker room where women often don't feel welcome even when they know how to play; height, business suits, and deep voices convey authority; speaking with little emotion in one's voice and without tag questions is a sign of articulateness and assurance.

Oppressions experienced by queer people are entirely a result of processes of normalization. In our societies heterosexual orientation and gender behavior conformity do not simply function as norms in the sense of the way the majority of people are. The society holds up heterosexual desire as normative in the sense of better in a vast number of ways that queer literature, film, and theory have revealed and that straight society hardly even notices until it is challenged. Respect and equality under these circumstances cannot mean that each sees the others as like themselves, but rather a respect for differences in ways that will not disadvantage. Ideals of impartiality and neutrality, I have repeatedly argued, tend to assume default social norms that position some people as deviant. When people who are different in one or another way attempt to conform to those norms, they often fail. And if the norm should become expansive enough to include some of them, the process of normativity continues to position some people as deviant. Thus, for example, some gay couples may try to conform to the norms of respectability dominant in straight society: monogamous coupling with one or two children, inviting straight friends to dinner parties, and so on. Queers who do not wish to live this way then become further stigmatized. Rather than expand application of a single standard to try to include everyone, it is more just and respectful to acknowledge difference and accept plural forms of life (Warner, 2000).

Important forms of racial and ethnocentric domination, finally, exhibit the injustice of normalization. Consider Latinos in America. The United States continues to define itself as an English speaking country, even as the number of its native Spanish speaking citizens and permanent residents rises to almost one-fifth. The normativity of English disadvantages and stigmatizes fellow Americans, and it is intended to do so. Bi-lingual education in Spanish and English has all but disappeared in the United States, and is even ruled illegal in some districts. The primary injustice this produces is disadvantage and extra burden: Spanish speaking children with just as much native intelligence and enthusiasm as their English speaking neighbors must learn mathematics and history under the serious handicap of less comprehension of English.[5]

Although anti-Black racism has many sources and interactive dynamics even after explicit discrimination has been outlawed, processes of normalization have a part in them. The norms of speech and comportment that the dominant society associates with intelligence, respectability, trustworthiness, and ingenuity are more typically of whites than African Americans. When African Americans walk, talk, laugh and shake hands like brothers and sisters in Black communities in integrated professional settings, they are often perceived warily by the whites there.

In sum, normalization concerns the way that the physical and mental capacities, cultural styles, or ways of living typical of particular social segments are held as a standards according to which everyone's attributes or behavior are evaluated. What is 'normal' in the sense of typical of a majority of persons, or typical of a dominant group, shifts into a standard of what is good or right. Those who for reasons not of their own making do not fit the standard become positioned as lesser or inferior. As a result they tend to be stigmatized, put at unfair disadvantage in accessing benefits, or excluded from participation in major institutions on an equal basis. Many have thought in the past and continue to think that the remedy for this problem of injustice is to construct more neutral standards. I will not say that this is always impossible, but it is often problematic. People's bodies and bodily capacities are different enough, for example, that any assumption of a single normative body will stigmatic and disadvantage some. On a different issue, there is no such thing as a neutral language of speech pattern. Only the explicit acknowledgment that these differences among people exist, and a commitment to accommodate to them so that everyone will be able equally to achieve well being and respect can responds to the demands of justice.

## IV. Democratic Inclusion

A third issue of justice not reducible to distribution has to do with decision making power. People obliged to follow rules or abide by decisions when they have had no opportunity to participate in their formulation frequently claim that they have been done an injustice. Democratic practices rectify such injustice. Several of the essays in this symposium attend to issues of difference and democracy, and the schooling of citizens for democracy.

Ronald Beiner's essay is most centrally concerned with the implications of a politics of difference for democratic community. He believes that democratic citizenship requires that members of a society have a shared sense of community and mutual identification, and that difference threatens the solidarity necessary for liberal equality to be institutionalized. Referring only to a single article of mine, first published in 1989, Beiner claims that the politics of difference I have theorized rejects any kind of universalist moral commitments. He also says that I assert that persons who are members of different social groups fundamentally cannot understand each other. Given such a rejection of universalism and the ability of people to communicate, he suggests that my main theory contradicts my also stated commitment to democratic inclusion.

If my writings did indeed take the positions Beiner attributes to them, he would be correct that a politics of difference cannot be consistent with inclusive democratic process. Fortunately, several of the other papers in the symposium cite passages and explain ideas that show that Beiner's portrait is distorted. Enslin and Frazer have both well summarized the argument about communication across differentiated structural positions which is at the core of my recent book, *Inclusion and Democracy*. Coalitions and solidarities must be built from the differences of value and privilege that divide members of a society. To build them, a democratic process must first ensure that members of relatively disadvantaged groups have opportunities to express their experiences, needs, and opinions in situations where differently situated others can hear. In situations of structural inequality, this usually requires taking affirmative steps to include and represent socially and economically disadvantaged groups. My essay, 'Asymmetrical Reciprocity', which is the focus of Simone Galea's contribution to this symposium, argues precisely that differently situated persons *can* understand one another. To do so, however, they often need to suspend the assumption that they are *like* one another, or that understanding another person means identifying with them.

Eisenberg quotes a passage from *Justice and the Politics of Difference* in which I explicitly endorse the universalist claim that all individuals are of equal moral worth and all should be able to participate in economic and political relations of society. In 'Polity and Group Difference', I argue that universalism in this sense is often not well served by formally equal rights that treat everyone in the same way. Frazer refers to another distinction I make in *Inclusion and Democracy*, between a *community*, in which people share norms and ways of life, and a polity, which entails a weaker unity among its members. To understand themselves in the same polity, I suggest, means that persons understand that they dwell together within social relations that affect them all, where some of their problems are shared, and that they recognize themselves to be governed by a common set of rule making and negotiating procedures.

Several of the writers here, including Enslin, Beiner, and Eisenberg, recommend more robust socialization for participation in public processes of a democratic state as one of the main tasks of an educational system. Frazer endorses this, but argues that such civic education is not sufficient for democratic justice. Citizens ought also to learn how to engage in democratic struggle, she suggests; good citizens should not merely know the rules, cast informed votes, and try to hold their elected leaders accountable. They ought also to be ready to bring conflict and difference into public and work through them.

I agree with Frazer, as well as with the others who here recommend active political education. I am struck, however, by the fact that the writers in this symposium seem to assume that democratic practices concern the sphere of government primarily. Issues of justice in decision making extend beyond public policy, however. As Michael Walzer illustrates in his story of garbage collectors in San Francisco, democracy in the workplace can do much to elevate the meaning and status of nonprofessional work (Walzer, 1983). When many corporate decisions have consequences that profoundly affect the lives of many people, economic democracy becomes a *claim* of justice, even if it should turn out after examination that it is not a well grounded claim for some circumstances (Shapiro, 1999).

## V. Difference as Cultural Expression

My own early work on the politics of difference was inspired by movements for equality and inclusion in advanced industrial democratic societies—the feminist movement, movements of African Americans, American Indians, gay and lesbian movements, movements of people with disabilities. The marginalized groups mobilized by each of these movements labored under stigma and disrespect prompted by their perceived difference from a mainstream. All had discovered, however, that their struggles for equal respect were not always well served by policies that claimed to treat them in the same way as those in dominant groups. Partly as a result of the devaluation of forms of life and modes of being with which many members of each of these groups shared affinities, moreover, each argues that some of their stigmatized differences should be reconceived as positively valuable.

Much recent political theory taking up issues of politics in relation to group difference has focused on other sorts of groups: cultural and religious groups making liberty claims more than equality claims. Amish people in the U.S., Orthodox Jews and Muslims in Europe and North America, and ethnic minorities in many societies claim rights to freedom of cultural expression in public and have resisted policies to pressure their assimilation to the dominant culture and/or to restrict their cultural practices.

The value of tolerance is at stake in these debates more than that of inclusion in a diversely interacting public. Many of these groups seek separation more than participation. In many cases, of course, members of these groups wish to maintain cultural specificity at the same time as they have equal opportunity to compete for winning positions in the capitalist competition. To the extent that they do, their claims involve equality issues. I think that it is important nevertheless to distinguish between a politics of difference that arises primarily from difference in national culture or religion, on the one hand, and difference that arises primarily from structural relations in sexuality, division of labor, or the deviance of kinds of bodies, on the other.

Of course, each of these can produce the other. The cultural difference of Pakistanis in England underlies a racialization of their relation to others that subjects them to structural inequality. The marginalization and stigma suffered by people with disabilities or African Americans motivates them to form solidarities that create new and positive forms of cultural expression. Cultural majorities often confine members of cultural minorities to specific social positions, and people positioned in similar ways in social structures often forge new sub-cultures. The dynamics of exclusion and the claims of justice nevertheless are often distinct.[6]

Avigail Eisenberg asks what the politics of difference as I have theorized it implies for religious difference. She argues that opening the doors to religious difference in public institutions can conflict with the objective of having an inclusive heterogeneous public. Ronald Beiner makes similar points. Neither writer appears to see a distinction between cultural difference and difference grounded in structures of work, sexuality and embodied normativity. The tensions they find between respecting difference and promoting a heterogeneous public may be mitigated if we understand the specificity of recognition claims of various groups. In liberal democratic societies, some groups seek toleration of their distinct cultural practices. Others seek to remove their stigmatized or devalued social position which derives from their perceived deviation from a norm. Responding to each claim justly requires accepting diversity, but in different ways.

Some groups, often religious groups, make a third kind of claim: that their beliefs about the proper ideas or behavior of some persons should be generally ruling norms. Religiously based claims that only men and women should be allowed to marry or that women should not have equal status with men in professional or political positions have this form. It is these sorts of claims, I submit, rather than claims for denormalization or for cultural respect, which conflict with goals of equality and inclusion. It is one thing, for example, for Muslim fathers to claim the right of their daughters to wear head scarves to school, and another for them to claim that women in general, and their daughters in particular, should not have equal education with men.

I do not have space here fully to articulate and justify these distinctions, and explore their political implications. With these remarks I intend more to open questions for further research rather than to settle arguments. In conducting this research, I suggest, we should begin with the assumption that there are several categories of difference and recognition claims alive in contemporary liberal democratic politics, rather than assume more parsimoniously that they all have the same basic logic.

With this I conclude my response to this rich, diverse and intellectually stimulating symposium. These papers show that educational institutions and education policy are central for disputes about equality and difference.

### Notes

1. David Miller constructs a defense of the distributive paradigm against my criticisms, though he concedes that decision making power is an issue of justice not reducible to distribution; see Miller, 1999, pp. 14–18; Ian Shapiro agrees that focus on distribution is too narrow because it tends to obscure power as an issue of justice; see Shapiro, 1999, especially pp. 232–233.
2. John Rawls, for example, repeatedly notes that his theory of justice imagines a society with persons that have a 'normal range' of capacities (see Rawls, 1993).
3. See, for example, Kittay (1999).
4. I have detailed the strains produced by this imperative of secrecy in my essay, 'Menstrual Meditations,' forthcoming in Young, 2004.
5. I have focused on structural injustice done to Latinos in my paper, Structure, Difference, and Hispanic: Latino claims of justice, in: Jorge J. E. Gracia and P. de Greiff (eds) Hispanics/ Latinos in the United States (New York, Routledge, 2000), pp. 147–166.
6. As I said above, my earliest work on the politics of difference was more concerned with structural differences than issues of cultural toleration and repression. Critical responses to that earlier work by theorists such as Nancy Fraser and Brian Barry have helped me see that

contemporary theorists tend to blend various claims of group based justice. In the meantime, my own work has also moved to consider issues of the self-determination of peoples and how differentiated peoples can dwell together, in addition to my continued concern with the inequalities engendered by structural differences of gender, racialist, sexuality, and ability. On the former set of issues, see, Young, 1995, 2001a, 2001b.

## References

Kittay, E. V. (1999) *Love's Labor: Essays on women, equality, and dependency* (London, Routledge).

Miller, D. (1999) *Principles of Social Justice* (Cambridge, MA:, Harvard University Press).

Rawls, J. (1993) *Political Liberalism*, Lecture I (New York, Columbia University Press).

Shapiro, I. (1999) *Democratic Justice* (New Haven, Yale University Press).

Young, I. M. (1995) Together in Difference: Transforming the logic of group politics conflict, in: W. Kymlicka, (ed.), *The Rights of Minority Cultures* (Oxford, Oxford University Press).

Young, I. M. (2000a) *Justice and the Politics of Difference* (Princeton, NJ, Princeton University Press).

Young, I. M. (2000b) Disability and the Definition of Work, in: L. Pickering Francis & A. Silvers, *Americans With Disabilities: Exploring Implication of the Law for Individuals and Institutions* (New York, Routledge).

Young, I. M. (2001a) Equality of Whom? Social groups and judgments of injustice, *Journal of Political Philosophy*, 9:1.

Young, I. M. (2001b) Two Concepts of Self-Determination, in: A. Sarat & T. Kearns, (eds), *Human Rights* (Ann Arbor, University of Michigan Press).

Young, I. M. (forthcoming) Menstrual Meditations, in: I. M. Young, *On Female Body Experience* (New York, Oxford University Press).

Walzer, M. (1983) *Spheres of Justice* (New York, Basic Books).

Warner, M. (2000) *The Trouble with Normal* (Harvard, Harvard University Press).

# Notes on Contributors

**Ronald Beiner** is a Professor of Political Science at the University of Toronto. His books include *Political Judgment* (1983), *What's the Matter with Liberalism?* (1992), *Theorizing Citizenship* (1995), *Philosophy in a Time of Lost Spirit* (1997), *Theorizing Nationalism* (1999), and *Liberalism, Nationalism, Citizenship* (2003). He has also edited Hannah Arendt's *Lectures on Kant's Political Philosophy* (1982).

**Avigail Eisenberg** is an Associate Professor of Political Science at University of Victoria in Canada. She is the author of *Reconstructing Political Pluralism* (SUNY, 1995), and co-editor of *Minorities within Minorities* (Cambridge University Press, 2005) as well as several articles on accommodating multinationalism and multiculturalism in liberal states. She is currently working on a book about minorities and identities.

**Penny Enslin** is Professor of Education in the Faculty of Humanities at the University of the Witwatersrand, Johannesburg. She teaches philosophy of education, with particular interest in democracy and citizenship education. Her recent publications have focused on peace education, the educational implications of South Africa's Truth and Reconciliation Commission, Africanist approaches to citizenship education, and higher education.

**Elizabeth Frazer** is Official Fellow and Tutor in Politics, New College, Oxford and Lecturer in Politics in the Social Studies Division at the University of Oxford. She is the author of *Problems of Communitarian Politics: unity and conflict* (Oxford University Press, 1999), and has written a number of articles on political education. She is currently working on the theoretical question of 'what politics ought to be'.

**Simone Galea** is a lecturer at The University of Malta where she teaches philosophy of education, feminist theories and qualitative research methods. Her current research interests bring all these together to focus on teachers' formation of their philosophies of education. She has recently completed her doctoral studies at The Nottingham Trent University with a feminist genealogical study of teachers as mothers.

**Sharon Gewirtz** is Professor of Education and a member of the Centre for Public Policy Research at King's College London. Her research and teaching interests are in the sociology of education and education policy. She has a particular interest in social justice.

**Mitja Sardoč** is researcher at the Educational Research Institute in Ljubljana, Slovenia, where he is currently engaged in research projects on citizenship education, school autonomy, inclusion and equal educational opportunities. His research focuses on political theory and philosophy of education. He has edited a number of journal special issues on citizenship education and has interviewed some of the most renowned contemporary political philosophers on the topic of education and political theory, including Michael Walzer, Iris Marion Young, and Martha C. Nussbaum.

He is Executive Editor of *Theory and Research in Education* and chief regional editor for Europe of the *Journal of Citizenship & Teacher Education.*

**Iris Marion Young** is Professor of Political Science at the University of Chicago. Her most recent book is *Inclusion and Democracy* (Oxford University Press, 2000). In 2005 Oxford University Press will issue a collection of her essays under the title, *On Female Body Experience: Throwing Like a Girl and Other Essays.*

# Index